THE NET RESULT IS

Myles McDonough, 1973

THE NET RESULT IS

THE FLEXCON STORY

Myles McDonough

as told to Jack Galvin

TIDEPOOL PRESS
Cambridge, Massachusetts

TidePool Press
6 Maple Avenue, Cambridge, Massachusetts 02139
www.tidepoolpress.com

For information, address:
TidePool Press
7 Front Street, Maynard, Massachusetts 01754

Printed in the United States

Library of Congress Cataloging-in-Publication Data

McDonough, Myles J., 1929-2012
    The Net Result Is: The FLEXcon Story
    p.cm.
    ISBN 978-0-9914523-3-0
    1. McDonough, Myles J. 2. Worcester (Mass.)—Biography
    3. Corporate History—FLEXcon—Spencer 4. Memoir
    I. Title.

    2016948093

To my wife and partner, Jean

Myles' Irish Soda Bread

Prep. Time: 25 minutes

Cooking Time: 45 minutes @ 325°

- 2 cups flour
- 1/3 cup sugar
- 2 teaspoons of baking powder
- 1 teaspoon of baking soda (optional)
- 1 cup raisins
- 2 tablespoons caraway seed
- Pinch of salt
- 3/4 cup of milk

Put into meat loaf pan—½ the height—if pan too large (long) shorten by aluminum foil. Grease pan with Crisco or Wesson oil before using in order to remove bread easily after baking cycle. When taken from oven, turn over on wire grate and remove pan.

Note:
1) Sift flour (very important)
2) Mix all dry ingredients, then add raisins, then add milk
3) May be toasted—may use butter on toasted or untoasted bread
4) May be frozen
5) May be served ½ hour after removal from oven

TABLE OF CONTENTS

Introduction   IX

Childhood and Education   I

Early Career   19

FLEXcon Begins   37

Innovations   51

Connections   71

Expansion   87

The 100 Million Dollar Goal   103

Impressions & Memories of Myles   109

FLEXcon 60 Years   123

Acknowledgements   143

Myles and Jean McDonough, 1982

INTRODUCTION

A eulogy by friend and colleague, Richard Silverman
April 9, 2012

THE DAY AFTER Myles McDonough died, March 30, 2012, Jean
called me and I agreed to do the eulogy. The next day she called
again and said she had just spoken to the priest at the church
where the funeral was to take place. He wanted to know how old I
was and she told him. He insisted that I write my eulogy and read
it at the Mass. Apparently he had experience with octogenarians.
They do tend to forget. When I stood before the congregation, I
couldn't believe the multitude I was facing. Every seat was filled
and people were standing in the back and along the sides of the
seated congregation. I later heard the service was broadcast to
an overflow crowd in the basement. Over 800 people had come
to pay their respects to Myles. I was SO glad that I was able to
read my prepared notes. Stage fright might have taken over. My
original notes follow:

When Jean called to tell me of Myles passing, I couldn't believe
it. My good friend of sixty years was gone. I had spoken to him

the day before he died and we talked of our upcoming forum meeting. Our forum was a monthly meeting of twelve guys who have nothing in common except for their masculine sex and their membership in the Young Presidents Organization. Many, many years ago when we all ran companies, we discussed business problems. Now our forum members talk about our grandchildren and the various pills that we take.

The other topic that Myles and I discussed was a prospective dinner. This was to be with our mutual Worcester friends, Tommy and Dick Dearborn. We discovered this would have to be a lunch instead of a dinner—not one of the six of us drives at night. I want to point out that I seem to retain old friendships. While my relationship with Myles is 60 years old, Tommy McNeil Dearborn and I met in kindergarten eighty-four years ago.

Sixty years ago, I was passing the office of our company's purchasing agent. I was called in to meet a new salesman. His name was Myles McDonough and he was trying to sell us chemicals or adhesives. Our agent pointed out that he didn't think we could use Myles' products and asked me for my opinion. I asked Myles to come into my office and after listening to his sales pitch, I asked for samples of a clear coating that I thought we could use to prevent tarnishing of our tinsel ribbons. I liked Myles and told him that we'd have lunch on his next call. Very frankly, I liked his sales ability and thought be might be a good prospect for our sales force.

At our next meeting, over a corned beef sandwich, I heard about his background and future plans. He had worked his way through college. He had a night job with Sears, Roebuck. After graduation, he was offered a sales job in New England and most of the products in his line were for the many shoe factories that were then in our states. He heard a lot of the foremen in these shoe operations were Jewish, as were a number of the owners. The few old Jewish men that he knew in the New York area conversed with each other in Yiddish. He figured he would be one up on his competition. Before he set out on his first trip, he learned to speak fluent Yiddish. He was a most unique Irishman—he could speak English, French, Latin, Gaelic ... and Yiddish. Then Myles told me of his plan to move into his territory. I suggested Newton because of its fine school system, but he said he couldn't afford Newton and settled on a small house in Natick.

A year later, on one of his sales calls, Myles met Roger, an inside man in a coating company. They decided to start a company of their own. The two of them put a few bucks together and bought some junked old machinery. They made a coating machine from the junk, Roger ran it and sold its output. Years later, Myles bought out Roger, and Myles and Jean became the sole owners of FLEXcon—the name is short for Flexible Converting.

FLEXcon thrived and our friendship matured. One day I asked Myles if his annual turnover had reached a million dollars. He said they had just reached this milestone. I said, "you are now going to join the Young Presidents Organization." To be a candidate for this illustrious group, you had to have been made president of your company before your 39th birthday, have fifty employees and, at that time, have an annual volume of $1 million. I believe the minimum annual volume today is over eight million dollars. You must retire from YPO at age 50. However you can then join a senior group with the prestigious name of "World Presidents Organization."

When Myles told Jean about YPO, she was enthused because she had read about this organization and felt it would beneficial if Myles became a member, However, we had a problem. Myles called and said he got the application and FLEXcon only had 32 employees. I said, "How many of them are your salesmen?" He replied, "We can't afford to put our own men on the road. We sell through manufacturers' reps." I said, "How many reps have you got around the country?" "Twenty-two," was the answer. I said, "You have a total of 52 employees. Now send in the application." Sandy and I gave Myles and Jean a "welcome in" cocktail party and they became members of the New England chapter of YPO.

The McDonoughs attended many YPO lectures and took lots of YPO trips. We went to Hawaii, Mexico, England, Ireland and the Mediterranean countries together. They formed close friendships with other YPO couples. Two of their new friends were Ann and Bill Arthur, fellow Worcester residents. For my 60th birthday, the McDonoughs hired a yacht and took the Arthurs and the Silvermans for a ten-day cruise of the Outer Grenadines. The yacht had been owned by the King of Sweden, and the new owners, a sea captain and his wife, sailed it from Sweden to the Caribbean. It was available for charter once a year. Certainly, this was the best birthday gift I ever received. The McDonoughs attended our daughter's wedding and we went to their sons' weddings. Social events by either family were celebrated together.

Myles and I both believed in higher education for our families. I started small funds for my nine college-bound grand nieces and nephews. On the other hand, Myles paid the full college tuition for 26 of his relatives. Myles was always thinking of others. When he could no longer drive, he hired a limo service to take Jean and ourselves to the senior WPO meetings. He always gave the driver a few greenbacks to "go out and have some coffee while you wait for us." Whenever his driver took him to our monthly forum meetings and before Myles came in to the meeting, he always ordered lunch for his driver. I've heard that Myles was a great boss at FLEXcon and his employees had top benefits.

At a forum meeting, I complained to Myles, "My hands are getting arthritic ... and I have a hard time buttoning my shirts." Myles said, "You can see how bad my hands are ... I haven't been able to use my fingers for years." A few days later, I received a strange metal contraption in my mail. It was from FLEXcon. I called Myles and he told me it was a unique button hook that he had developed. Anyone with arthritic fingers could easily button a garment and he wanted me to have this assistance.

At another forum meeting, I told the group about a book I had just written. It was called *Soldier Boy* and detailed my experiences during World War II. Myles told me he'd have it printed and bound at FLEXcon. Deb Snow, executive assistant, was in charge of my job. She even had a cover designed and several hundred copies went out to friends.

At still another forum meeting, I told the group that I had heard that our fellow YPOer, Eliot Mover had gone bankrupt, not just his company but he personally had been on all the company notes, and now he didn't have enough money to buy food. I said I was going to send him a monthly check and Myles said he would match whatever I sent and he did. We both sent these checks until Eliot died.

Myles was proud of his wife and two sons. Jean handled the FLEXcon finances for many years. In the early days, she knew which suppliers banked her checks on the day they were received and which ones banked them a week later. Checks were sent out last to those suppliers who gave FLEXcon a little breathing room. Jean didn't let any cash sit idly in a bank account. She invested every penny she could and was in touch with investment opportunities all over the country. One year she made 21% on FLEXcon's idle cash and Myles said she was making a better return than he made on the company's product sales. Jean was also in charge of McDonough philanthropic gifts and there were many around Worcester.

The true miracle of FLEXcon's growth is how a company that is now doing hundreds of millions of dollars a year could operate and grow without any outside support or without borrowing a penny from a bank. This secret has never been divulged.

When older son Mark McDonough wanted to do his own thing, he started several companies, successfully sold them, and instead of retiring at an early age, he now has about seven restaurants on the north shore. Myles bragged of Mark's accomplishments.

When son Neil took over as president of FLEXcon, I'm not sure that Myles felt he himself could be easily replaced. He soon saw what a great job Neil was doing and for the last five years, Myles didn't go near FLEXcon. Neil was a fine executive and didn't need Myles looking over his shoulder. Wait a minute, that's not quite true. Myles went to the plant once a year so that he could get his free flu shot. Even as Chairman of the Board, Myles conducted all meetings at his home and not at FLEXcon.

Our last conversation together covered one other subject. He said he would bake a new batch of Irish soda bread and bring several loaves to our next meeting. Myles had been supplying me with this delicacy for a long time. I will miss my bread delivery tomorrow but to a far greater extent I will miss seeing one of the best friends that I ever had.

Myles in the kitchen making his famous Irish soda bread, c. 1980

Myles with his mother, c. 1933

1

CHILDHOOD AND EDUCATION

YOU COULD SAY that my first son Mark's birth and the birth of my company happened the same day. In that order. Picture a young wife in a hospital bed, exhilarated, exhausted, holding her newborn son in her arms and her husband comes in and says, "I'm quitting my job and I'm going to start my own business!"

Well, maybe not as dramatic as that. The hospital room scene makes for a good story, but the reality was a bit more practical. Actually Jean, who handled all of our money, had saved over $10,000. We had half the house paid for and most of our furniture bought, thanks to our envelope system of budgeting. I knew exactly what I was going to do. We had discussed the idea of going into business, but I must admit that the timing of my announcement was a surprise to Jean.

One thing is true: If I hadn't started then, I might never have. I found a willing and able partner, Roger Plourde, and I had a lot of ideas on how to take advantage of the new direction I saw business taking, particularly in the field I knew best. It was 1956;

I was 26 years old, full of energy, vision, and a willingness to work hard. When I saw Jean holding our new son I had already made up my mind. Otherwise the $10,000 could have easily been eaten up by the demands of a family. That might sound selfish, as if I were taking the food from my child to go on an adventure that had no guarantee of success, but I hope to show you in these pages how FLEXcon, our family business, grew from that decision. I want to show you how all the hard work that led to the development of FLEXcon's success has always provided me with the deepest satisfaction and, most of all, great fun. Indeed, FLEXcon became my life.

What gave me the idea that I could quit my job and start a new business, just as my family was growing? To answer that question I will have to bring you back to my own childhood. Imagine the following scenes:

> A small farmhouse, thatched roof, white stucco walls. In the large kitchen a young boy, four years old, stretches out dozing before the fire place, snuggled up against the warm breathing body of a baby lamb. It too lay still, exhausted from the long day of being separated from its mother, lost in the drizzle of the damp November gloom. The boy, equally tired, has been out in the fields, trotting to keep up with his grandfather, the two searching for the baby lamb. Now hours later, the baby lamb, found as it brayed in its tiny panicked voice, and the boy, are both warmed by the fire. Soothed by the voices of his mother and grandparents as they sit at the kitchen table and talk in low voices, the boy breathes in the wet smell of the baby lamb's woolly coat and clutches a curly crinkled tuft of it in his small fists. Tomorrow he will play in his barn, watch his grandfather fix the fence, chase the goslings, learn his numbers from his aunt, and listen to stories from his mother.

It is County Galway, Ireland, 1933. I am the small boy. I have come to Ireland with my mother to live with my grandparents. I will live here for three years in a farmhouse without electricity, without indoor toilets, in the quiet of the Irish countryside. I will learn so much at that kitchen table from aunts and uncles who eagerly want to teach me. Everyday is a school day, but I don't know it as that. I know it as the fun of learning.

But now as I lay before the fire, seeing the orange flashes of light behind my closed eyelids, and feeling the rhythm of the lamb's breathing, I am content in a moment that will stay with me always, to remind me of the Ireland of my childhood.

My mother and I were in Ireland because we had nowhere else to go. I'll explain. My mother and father, both Irish immigrants, had lived in Jersey City, New Jersey. My father was a hard worker, supplementing his carpentry job, as a weekend longshoreman on the Hoboken docks with other Irishmen. He saved enough to own two houses by the time he was twenty-nine and spent his free time singing and playing the accordion. In 1929, three months before I was born, he fell into the hold of a ship and died. In a time of low incomes, he had been saving enough to buy two cars, one for himself and one for his brother. They were delivered on the day of his funeral.

Unfortunately, after his death the McDonoughs, whom I would not meet until I was eighteen, did not treat my mother very well. My father had the houses and the insurance in his name, so his family was able to latch onto most of the proceeds and we were out of luck. My mother and I eventually moved in with her sister on Long Island, but with her husband tragically dead before the birth of their son, no money, home, or hope, my mother decided to go back to Ireland when I was two. There we were surrounded by relatives and I was "home-schooled" you might say, because I was learning at that kitchen table every day. It was a wonderful life for a young boy. I could run and play in the fields of our old-fashioned farm near Galway. One souvenir I still wear from that time was the result of a fall from the top of a pyramid of peat. Peat was, and still is, used for fuel in Ireland. It's dug from the damp ground and dried into hard bricks, very hard as I found out. When playing in the field one afternoon, I fell off the top of a pile of it and my front teeth were pushed up into my gums. Despite extensive dental work the teeth became permanently gapped into the lovely smile I wear to this day.

I guess I became a bit of a menace in Ireland. The goslings I cared for sometimes drowned, and I became too difficult to handle. By the time I was five, we were back on Long Island, so my mother could maintain my citizenship (not to mention that my grandfather had had his fill of me). It was not difficult for her to get her United States citizenship because we were the sort of Irish who spoke English, not Gaelic, and we had none of the other problems immigrants on the boat faced, such as illness and disease. My mother was much stronger on our return to America, having, "cried all my tears in Ireland," as she later told me.

I soon started school, but I found I was ahead of my peers, as I already knew how to read and do arithmetic. I became what you might call precocious or stubborn or whatever the hell it was. I would run home from school as soon as my mother brought me there. She put me in a carriage at the age of five to embarrass me,

Julia McDonough, c. 1929

but I didn't care. I hated the regimentation of American schools. I had been used to the independence of my Irish home-schooling, where all my relatives could give me what they remembered of their 5th grade educations. I was so far ahead of my peers when I came back that I answered all the teacher's questions before any of the others. I could do all the problems in my head! I guess I was very good at explaining concepts though, and I became the one who monitored the homework of my two older cousins at the kitchen table. In fact, I went through grammar school as a kind of mentor, taking care of the kids who had more difficulty learning. Otherwise I was bored out of my mind because, despite teachers' advice, my mother refused to move me up a grade. In my free time I took up Irish dancing to please my mother and, after kids teased me, took lessons to get rid of my brogue.

My mother's brother, Jim, became a substitute father for me. We moved in with him and his family in Highland Park, New Jersey when I was about seven. He gave us a room with a couch that folded out into a bed. My mother cleaned houses and eventually started working in the rectory. I would stop in after school and she'd always have a piece of cake or pie left over from the priests' dinner the night before. The priests ate well, and as a result, so did I. I hung around the rectory or played outside with my friends from the neighborhood while my mother worked hard inside. The pastor died in 1940. I remember because he had a 1939 Dodge, which seemed such a waste of a new car—funny what young boys consider important.

The replacement priest brought in his own housekeeper and our lives changed. My mother had strong hands from the farm in

The Geraghty family: (back row from left) *Jim,
Julia, John;* (front row) *Delia, Mary, c. 1950*

Ireland, so she began work in a new arsenal making ammunition
for the war. It was hard work and she had to ride the bus there,
often working the night shift, but she never complained. She
was just happy to be making money, and she had a plan, one
she kept secret. She wanted to buy a house. It was unheard of in
those days for a woman, a widow and single mother at that, to
get a mortgage. She discussed it over tea with her friend Mrs.

Myles, 1940

Delesandro, who often came over to get away from her grouch of a husband, and the two of them went to see a judge they knew for advice. After looking over her finances, the judge said by all means go for it, which she did. She didn't even tell her brother until it was final because she knew he would have vetoed the idea even more loudly had he known about it ahead of time. Even though Uncle Jim put up a fight, the net result was we had our own home. She even rented out an upstairs apartment to help pay for it. I learned a lot from my mother's example. She taught me to use whatever skills I had to create a good life for my family, which I did by creating a company she could be proud of.

My mother and I were happy to finally have our own home, two houses away from her brother's as it was. No longer did I have to share everything with my cousins. I had the place to myself, particularly when my mother worked at night. What greater pleasure could there be for a twelve year old than to listen to the radio, do a little reading, maybe some homework, then listen to the radio again, rattling around until just before my mother came home at 10:30 pm. I would jump into bed pretending to have been asleep, but she was crafty. She'd go to the tubes in the back of the radio, and they would give me away, because they were still warm. Something had to be done about the young Myles left to his own devices for all those hours. The solution: boarding school.

Mount Saint Michael's in New Rochelle, New York, to be exact. While I was away learning a new life under the Marist Brothers from France and Canada, I often wondered how life was for my mother. When I was at home she had at least had someone to deal with, to talk to, to be with, even though I was only a young boy. It was important to her though that I take advantage of this opportunity of being exposed to an education I would not have had if I stayed home with her.

To take advantage of opportunities, you must develop a broad vision, become creative, so that whatever you do in life becomes part of the process. One very important part of the process is the ability to think, alone, in quiet, for extended periods of time. I came upon this ability to think in a way few people know about: my high school years spent in the monastery. That's right. Myles

McDonough, the married father of two, the grandfather of seven, almost became a religious brother. I could have spent the rest of my life in quiet contemplation, praying, getting up at the crack of dawn, wearing a black robe, eating silent meals, and none of what I'm writing about here would have happened.

I was a good student at Mount Saint Michael's. My competitive sense to be number one in my class fueled my learning. For example, I'd go to chapel for prayer, my Missal open before me, eyes on the page, mouth moving as all the other boys. No one knew it, but hidden on those Missal pages were my class notes. I was determined to beat out the skinny kid with the highest math average. While everyone else prayed, I studied. And it worked. I was in the top three of my class. I knew a good deal when I saw one, and I realized I was getting one hell of an education at a very low cost. Well, at a pretty high cost to tell the truth, just not monetarily. Many hours of forced quiet, regimentation that made grammar school seem like the freedom of my Irish childhood, Latin translations, and Saturday night Gregorian chant choir rehearsals. Sounds like just the sort of fun any American teenager would crave, doesn't it? Well, actually I did. Maybe not crave it, but I knew the education was the best I could get no matter what I did. The habits, the discipline, the close work with teachers who were always available to help; I felt it was a very good trade off for a few years without girls. I had another motivation for my dedication as well.

The brothers had a junior seminary in Esopus on the Hudson, a converted mansion that must have been donated by some wealthy man, perhaps suddenly concerned about his soul. I was asked if

Marist Brothers retreat at Esopus

I wanted to join the brothers and go into the seminary. I would prepare to spend my life as a monastic and a teacher, starting in Esopus, then onto Saint Joseph's Novitiate and taking courses at Marist College in Poughkeepsie. Pretty heavy duty decisions for a fourteen year old so I talked it over with my mother. She was proud of me, proud that I was asked, as any Irish mother would be, but left the decision to me.

I said yes, I would go to Saint Joseph's. My initial reason for accepting sounds very naïve now. I was going to get my mother into heaven. Pray her way there, I guess. I would live in such a way that those gates had to open for her. I didn't think then, as I often did later, that she didn't need any help from me. I was willing to spend my life in monastic quiet to ensure my mother's place in heaven. At first, that motivation was enough for me, but the truth is I always wanted to be a big wheel, the guy in charge, number one. After a year or so in the mansion on the Hudson, I knew being a teacher would never be enough for me. I knew then, that I had to leave, seek out another way to get my mother into heaven.

Twenty degrees, a bitter wind, stars stabbing the black sky. Across the river, the twinkling lights of a town, homes, warm and inviting. A solitary figure walks past the chapel, fingering beads. It is silent rosary time. The young boy hunched into his heavy coat is not thinking of the Joyful Mysteries, but how he will make his way in the world; how he will provide for his mother, the woman who has made his life the center of hers, who works for nothing more or less than his success. He knows he won't stay though. He will instead use what this place has taught him to provide for his mother here on earth. He will ensure that she will have all that she needs to live an easier life, that in her later years she will not suffer the anxiety of so many widows as they age, that he will be able to take care of her as she has done for him. He will tell the brothers soon that he will leave after this year, but that they will not be sorry for him to go. He will be back in years ahead with money to help them. He thinks all this as he walks the grounds of the monastery. He has grown used to thinking, alone, in the quiet, where he finds comfort in the rich silence of time ticking, which has taught him to string together the ideas and thoughts which will be with him his whole life. Not the specific thoughts of this cold night, but the ability to use islands of time to think, as one might weave straw, slowly, carefully, contentedly, by the hour.

Even now, at night when my wife Jean is reading, I can sit for two hours and just think. These are times when I like to be alone. Before I retired from FLEXcon, I would use this time to reconsider something I was working on or come up with a new idea to pass on. When I hit a wall, these two-hour think sessions would give me an opportunity to come up with at least a hint of an answer, a technique that I had developed out of those early years in the monastery.

I told my mother on my summer break that I was leaving the brothers after my senior year. The Irish mother, proud to have her son in a religious order, had only praise for my decision. The brothers, of course, were disappointed, until I told them that I would be rich some day, and I would be back with a big donation, a promise I eventually came through on.

That same summer I finally met my father's relatives. My mother had never spoken of my father or his family. Every year on Memorial Day we would take a series of buses to spend an hour at his grave site in Arlington, New Jersey. We would travel two hours each way, but she never talked about him and, as a result, I never felt comfortable asking. All I had was the formal picture from their wedding. The stiff unsmiling pose photographers demanded in those days gave me few clues about this dark-haired, clear-eyed man. I do have an idea of what may have kept her quiet though. If she had opened up her heart about him, she perhaps would not have been able to swallow her resentment, her anger, maybe she felt that it would taint me and poison me towards life.

My father's sister Barbara called my mother asking to meet us, and my mother said, "For Myles' sake, I'll go." She was quietly cordial and polite as we met with my father's brother, who had opened a bar in Jersey City years before, and his family. It wasn't until later that I understood the significance of that meeting and its underlying tension. One of my cousins explained to me how his relatives had not treated my mother well after my father died.

There were matters of insurance and the ownership of the house that the McDonoughs were able to take charge of and manipulate to their own ends. My mother had been left without many financial resources. Aunt Barbara wanted to clear the air and bring us all together again, and for a while we were closer. In fact, my cousin Joe was in my wedding party. Occasionally I'd stop into the bar in Jersey City to see his father, my uncle. I even stayed at my cousin's place one night. Going to bed that night I saw a pistol sticking out from underneath his pillow. Living near Journal Square was much more of an adventure than I wanted. As you might imagine, that was the only night I ever stayed there. After I married and moved to Massachusetts we got together less frequently though.

The point I want to make about all of this is my mother's wisdom. For all those years she never once railed to me about the McDonoughs and her treatment at their hands, never once passed on to me any legacy of hate or even disappointment. She was not a bitter woman. She got on with her life, preserving both of us from the frustrated anger that resentment can feed. I never had a father and therefore did not miss mine. What I had was a mother who gave me all of herself and kept me whole and positive, refusing to let resentment determine our lives.

Julia at Myles and Jean's wedding, 1951

After leaving the monastic life as a teen that summer, I decided I wanted to go to Rutgers, but I was too late in applying and told to wait until the next semester. I was desperate to go to college, but I knew my chances of admission would be slim if I waited because of all the returning veterans, so I went to Seton Hall, transcript in hand, two days before classes were to begin. The admissions office was impressed with my marks, particularly on the Regents Diploma exams, yet could not offer any help. Too late, but they suggested I look around the campus to see if I'd like to come the next semester. As I was walking around I came upon the swimming pool and struck up a conversation with a tall older man toweling off. We talked about my rejection and my high marks and he said he'd look into it. We met in the admissions office an hour later, he in his collar and cassock, smiling and telling me I was in. It turned out that he was Monsignor Kelly, President of Seton Hall. A chance conversation, how about that for an opportunity!

Once enrolled, I had some trouble with my peers. Seton Hall was a blooming campus in 1946, made up of Quonset huts, new teachers, and teeming with returning veterans going to college under the GI Bill. Wheeler-dealer Monsignor Kelly did a great job of transforming the school from 1,200 before the war to over 5,000 students. Not all the returning soldiers were brilliant though; some had to cheat their way through. I took a physics course with some vets who were clever enough, as they saw it, to steal a naïve professor's exams. The young teacher, a medical school applicant, graded on a curve, so those blessed with foreknowledge got the As and Bs, sinking the rest of us to lower depths of the alphabet. Imagine going home to your mother and trying to explain how you got a K in physics. Not an F, but a K. And I was almost passing!

I had to pass that course somehow though. The next semester, I found a tough, cranky priest, an old son of a bitch, who made it clear you either did the work or you failed. Cheat and you were out. He was crafty enough to know if there was any cheating going on and the whole class realized it. He knew I was working and working hard though. Finally in that last month it all clicked. When I told my mother I had gotten an A in physics, I felt it was one of the happiest things I ever told her.

Competing in classes with cheating GI Bill vets didn't sit too well with me, so I decided to change the way I went to school. After finishing two years of Seton Hall, I switched to summer and night classes for three years. It was a very different atmosphere in those classes because we were all working and paying our way through the courses. I worked at Sears. I had learned a lot from my Uncle Jim, who was a machinist at Mack Truck. He had taught me all about carpentry and machines while we fixed things up around his house together. If I made a mistake he'd always make me rip it out and do it again. The net result was I became pretty good at using tools, which helped me on the job at Sears and I even fixed up a car, so I could drive out to Long Island and see my girlfriend Jean.

After two years of nights and weekends as a janitor at Sears, I had learned enough to be hired as a technician in chemistry at Johnson & Johnson, while still attending school at night, and working weekends as a salesman at Sears, in paints, appliances, and even automotive. My plan worked. I graduated on time with my class and received the grades I was looking for. I had also learned a valuable lesson: I found I could solve the problems I had with the vets and the courses by changing the way I approached college. I knew the evening students were working all day to pay for the opportunity to go to college. I wanted to be in that serious environment and made sure I got there.

Myles and Gerry Collette, 1962

2

Early Career

After I graduated from Seton Hall in 1950, I finally got a chance to go out and sell. The company Rubber and Asbestos (now National Starch and Chemical Company) sent me out to Brooklyn and the Bronx to sell adhesives to German Jewish people in the tire business. They were guys who took one look at an Irish kid with an innocent face—I was all of twenty-two—and told me to get lost. Would I go back to the lab, doing research, all day, every day though? No, years in the lab were not for me. I wanted to be out on the road where I could make some money. In research you might come up with a great idea which gets used, but then that's the end of it. The people who make the real money for the company, and therefore themselves, are the guys who get rid of products, the salesmen. I was good at selling, my years at Sears had taught me that, but I had to figure out a way to talk to those business owners in Brooklyn. Yiddish was the answer. I started taking lessons and found people to practice with. Soon, I'd walk into a retread place, and to their surprise,

Yiddish would come out of this Irish face. It worked, and I began getting phone calls and orders back at the office from thick accented guys looking for the Irish kid with the Yiddish *kuph*, or head.

While working for Rubber and Asbestos, I began attending Stevens Institute of Technology. I soon gave up my graduate work there to go to Rutgers for sales courses though. I realized Stevens, the MIT of New Jersey, was not for me. Sales was what I wanted, not lab work. Besides, the walk from the train to the Stevens campus was too much of an adventure for me. We had to walk in groups so bums wouldn't beat us up; that's what the neighborhood had come to. And the smell of coffee was so overwhelming from the manufacturing plant, it made us sick to our stomachs. Industries got away with all kinds of things in those days. Hoboken's smell of coffee was not bad compared to the pharmaceutical plants of New Brunswick, which gave off the perfume of penicillin, or Jersey City's refineries. The government didn't give a happy good Christ though. After all, we needed penicillin, needed coffee, needed fuel. So what if half of New Jersey stank?

Then it was on to New England. I married Jean in 1951 and got my first company car in 1952. I would eat breakfast at midnight, was on the road by 5:00 a.m. and in Boston by nine to make my first calls. I would work my way down from New Hampshire to Connecticut. I soon found out there were very few Irish businessmen in Boston though. There were, however, many Jewish businessmen. I met Sam Butman of Flextex Combining, recognized his accent and threw some Yiddish at him. He didn't

Myles and Jean, 1951

understand a word I said. He explained that the Jewish in Boston were mainly of Russian extraction, and only the German Jewish speak Yiddish. After that, Sam became a good customer and a good friend of mine, for one very important reason. I would come into his office on a Monday, and ask him about problems he might be having with our products. I always told him I would come up with a solution by the next week and I did: I'd come back with the adhesive he needed, for which he would be grateful, and place more orders.

That idea became the philosophy behind all my later business efforts: listen to the customer. See the problems from their point of view and try to solve them. It didn't take me long to figure out that if I could help them make money, I'd be helping myself. I would come into new places, ask about business, and ask about problems. Customers knew there would be no bullshit from me. They knew I could give them the numbers, make the drawings, because I knew the formulas. I had worked in the lab to make the adhesives, now I was selling what I had developed. They'd tell me a problem and I would have an answer for them; therefore a profitable answer for me.

Before I go on about starting the business I think it's time for a few basic ideas about plastics and what we learned to use at FLEXcon. Stay with me here, there will be a quiz at the end. There are two basic types of plastics: thermosets and thermoplastics. Thermosets are plastics that can cure (usually through heat) to a stronger form. In other words, thermosets, once cured, stay that way. They may start off as liquid, powder, or malleable before curing, but once the process is complete, thermosets are rigid and entirely heat resistant. Think Bakelite (which all electrical outlets were originally made of), melamine, epoxy resin or Duroplast, all plastics used in heat resistant products. These are not the products you will see at FLEXcon however. We use only thermoplastics, materials that can be deformed, melted, and reformed, in other words, plastics in the truest sense of the word. Mylar®, acetates, and vinyl are some examples. Thermoplastics respond to heat, or cold, and because of their flexibility can be used in many creative ways.

During one of my long think sessions I found a gap in the market. I started to realize that in the ten years since World War II, many new products, especially adhesives, plastics, and vinyl, had been exploding onto the scene. I also saw that many of the companies I called on were refusing to take on customers because they believed the jobs were too small to make a profit. I came up with one conclusion I could not shake: there were a lot of people, with great ideas, that I could help. If I was smart enough to create the stuff, in thermoplastic materials, needed to make their ideas a reality, I could go into business for myself.

I had already been exposed to the adhesives field during my time at Johnson & Johnson and Rubber and Asbestos. I knew that Dacron®, developed for parachutes during the war by Dupont, was gaining multiple new uses. Working at Permacel, a division of Johnson & Johnson, I saw new experiments and products developing pressure-sensitive tapes for customers. The whole time I was helping other people make money and develop their own companies. All my ideas were benefiting others. The more I thought about starting my own business the more urgent the idea became. After all, I was going on twenty-four. I had to get going.

Starting my own business was always on my mind. When I made my rounds of sales calls, I was on the look-out. Lunch hours in Fall River or New Bedford would find me scouring junkyards for potential parts to build the machine I had in mind. You'd be surprised at the treasures a junkyard can hold! On my lunch hours in the more wealthy Connecticut towns I listened to soap operas like "Stella Dallas" on the car radio, but not in Fall River or New Bedford. Those Massachusetts town junkyards offered adventure because the old mill machines ended up there. My Uncle Jim, in addition to kicking my ass when I needed it as a kid, had taught me a lot about how machines worked, along with my time in the automotive department at Sears, so I knew what to look for, vague as my plans were.

A friend of mine, Roger Plourde, was working for Multi-Color Corporation at the time. He was a year older than I and had been in the consulting business, but once I got him interested in pressure-sensitive products, he had risen pretty quickly at Multi-Color. We often had dinner together to talk business and the germ of the idea for FLEXcon started with those meetings, and also with the work Multi-Color was doing for DuPont.

Here's the quick version of a convoluted story: Multi-Color coated adhesives to Mylar®. One of their customers, DuPont, would send them adhesives made by their own people in Fairfield, Connecticut, to coat onto metalized Mylar® obtained from National Research for upholstery in cars for General Motors. Multi-Color was not happy with DuPont's small 1,500 yard orders though. They usually went for 100,000 yard orders, because it was a pain in the ass to stop machines, clean them, make sure they were cold, and then put in a new color for small orders, such as DuPont's. Besides, Multi-Color was becoming increasingly more interested in pressure-sensitive materials after watching the success of contact paper on the market. Contact paper was used to cover shelves, printed wood-grained or in colors, and could be made in big orders. Bill King, the president of Multi-Color, saw the potential and, because his father was a big wheel at Monsanto, he had a very good connection to the best of the new film techniques.

Now back to Roger and me at dinner. I told him, "I intend to go into business for myself very soon. Do you want to come along?" I wanted Roger because he knew the machines at Multi-Color and he had a good connection to Alan Dragone from National Research. If Multi-Color was no longer interested in DuPont, Roger would be of great help in both, getting us up and running, and snagging our first customer.

Roger was a bit hesitant, "You have to be very sure of yourself," he warned.

"I could not be surer of myself," I said, "I can sell anything we make and get the best prices. I have a lot of connection to the shoe trade wholesalers and I've been thinking about this Mylar."

He said he'd think about it, but I could tell his enthusiasm did not match mine. Here we were, 24 and 25, both young guys, starting families, but Roger was not as adventurous as I was. To me, starting a business was my goal. To him, it was a surprise. He came around though, and we agreed to go fifty-fifty.

I had confidence in taking on Roger as a partner because he knew the business and I knew the trade, and the people. I knew I could count on my customers to recommend me to others because wherever I went I successfully solved problems and helped businesses. Roger would be the inside guy, working the production; I'd be the outside guy, selling.

Then came the big decision. I told Jean I was definitely quitting my job, the day Mark was born, March 9, 1956. Even though we had long talked about it, this was the defining moment to move ahead. Not the best news a young mother could hear with her first child in her arms and the $10,000 she had worked hard to save now going down the dark empty hole of chance. Jean, I must tell you, was supportive, confident, and encouraging in every way she could be. There would be challenging times ahead for her. Eventually, she even hung her college diploma over the washing machine in our house in Natick to remind herself, her two young boys—Neil sixteen months younger than Mark—and a husband she hardly ever saw, that she did indeed have a brain, which she intended to use someday.

I don't want to paint too gloomy a picture though. I was about to take part in an adventure that would consume most of my waking hours for the next fifty years. I had the confidence, energy and vision to know I could make it, but if I did not, I told Jean, as she lay in that hospital bed holding Mark, "Don't worry. If I am not a success, I'll work for someone else and be the star. I'll tell them how to succeed and how not to screw it up."

Next we had to find a location. Spencer, Massachusetts, was a small town with an economy dependent on shoe manufacturing;

its population was French Canadian and Irish. It was not a town to screw around with. The French Canadians lived on one side of Main Street with the Irish on the other and the fights you would not believe. The town had a colorful past. Even Charles "Dutchy" Meloche, the chief of police in the 1940s, is said to have shot the tops off of the bottles behind the bars when he got a few drinks in him.

The Irish were not always welcome in Spencer. "Irish need not apply" signs were still visible in the 40s, but into this town the Irishman Myles came to start a business. French Roger and I chose Spencer because it was about an hour away from each of our homes, his to the west near Northampton, and me in Natick to the east. Also, Roger's in-laws, the Peloquins, lived there, owned the town beach, and knew many people. Not that Spencer welcomed us.

We found a building on Maple Street, owned by the guy who ran the grocery store, an empty garage; empty after the sailboat stored upstairs had been removed at least. We rented the upstairs, about 40 x 40 feet of unheated space. We went for the upstairs because the floor was smooth concrete, and once we installed a furnace downstairs, the upstairs got the best heat. Downstairs, by the way, was only open to the front. The back was on the side of a small hill so that eventually the rear of the garage, the place we used for pick-ups and deliveries, was the second story. At first, Roger was still working for Multi-Color and I still had my sales territory, so we worked on weekends and holidays beginning in March of '56.

Soon I had to tell Martin Grover, my boss at Rubber and

Maple Street garage, Spencer, Massachusetts, 2016

Asbestos that I was leaving to start my own company. Maybe because he was losing a good salesman or maybe he just really believed it, but he called me stupid to quit my job. When he knew I was serious though, he had me train a young new salesman, Bernie Alden. Bernie and I hit it off during those months of training, so much so that I would often visit him and his family at their home in Malden. Bernie later went on to become sales manager for Rubber and Asbestos. We always kept in touch, and years later we both wanted him to come join FLEXcon, but I had no place for him. Finally in 1977 our sales manager, Andy Hacanis, moved to Florida and I wanted Bernie to replace him in Spencer. Again I had to tell Martin Grover some bad news about one of his top guys. Martin was no happier about Bernie

Bernie Alden with Myles, c. 1990

leaving him than he was about me leaving when I quit twenty years before.

It was tough around Spencer in those early years. I was the better salesman, the guy who could talk to people, so I was designated to chase down workmen and open an account at the hardware store, but I was young, Irish, and new in town, so I couldn't get credit anywhere. The welder would demand payment, in cash, before he cut anything. The steel mills, where we bought a great deal of I-beam, the plumbing supply store, where we bought piping and other expensive materials, the Aubuchon Hardware Store, where we purchased nails, screws, and lumber—they all wanted cash. I'd hear, "I want the money first," and my answer was always, "Not a problem. How much?" and I'd pay cash, with a smile, no sense alienating the people we needed. We kept a shoebox where we'd put all our paid bills so we would know how much we had spent and how much we had left. That shoebox became basic to the FLEXcon philosophy, by the way. We kept the approach of always paying our way as we go, never driving ourselves into debt, always growing out of cash flow.

At first Roger and I put in $5,000 each to get the materials for the machine Roger had designed. Mr. Peloquin, Roger's father-in-law, became our best asset. He had been a machinist, so he taught me how to measure, how to drill, how to cut with the $35 electric saw he had me buy. I enjoyed working with Mr. Peloquin because he appreciated my efforts at learning all he had to offer.

Roger and I sweated our way through building our first machine, while most people were at the beach or spending time with their families that summer. You might think that after working all week as a salesman, then all day Saturday and Sunday on the machine, I would be tired by Monday morning, looking for at least one day off, but somehow I wasn't tired. In fact, I was energized by what we were doing. I only needed three or four hours of sleep then (and now) and was fascinated by the construction of the machine Roger had designed. Jean, of course, was at home with two kids, both under three, and I was away seven days a week. Although she was not happy about it, she never complained because she had faith in what had to be done. Jean had relatives in business—hardware stores, plumbing, restaurants—so she knew the commitment it took.

To build the machine we drilled into the floor, and then into the I-beams, holes exactly eighteen inches between each of the

Julia McDonough with Mark and Neil, 1960

three frames we had built. We wanted to be able to reverse the frames on either end, the reverse and rewind rolls, so we needed an exact distance. In the future we wanted to be able to either laminate or preheat the rolls first, so we made this one machine serve the purpose of two. We fed the steam heat from our furnace through a heat vent above the machine to make the Mylar® flexible, and further directed by a fan to evaporate the solvent from adhesives. We only had one motor involved to keep the tension in the roll steady, so there would be no dip in the roll, and we used car clutches to speed up the roll as it grew heavier on the cylinder. It was important to keep it tight. The middle cylinder, powered by the vari-drive motor, ran at a constant speed at no more than ten yards a minute. We had to control the speed because laminating needs a "dwell" time, so the two surfaces can marry. Embossing cold presented another challenge; we had to determine the appropriate speed of the machine to get the most use out of the roll.

Turns out all those lunch breaks spent in the junkyard were worth it. In Providence and New Bedford I found counters to lay out materials, and more importantly, rolls with ball bearings, which could be as expensive as the rolls themselves, from mills and manufacturing plants. It didn't take us long to find out that embossing rolls, that is rolls that would have specific designs imprinted on them, were the most expensive because they had to be custom made for a special pattern. In that case, the customer would pay for the roll which we would use. If we used the roll for another customer, and we would because after the pattern was out in the public it became more generic, the original customer would charge us 3% of what we had charged for the first year we used it, 2% for the second, and 1% for the third. For us, it would become maybe 2,000 yards for the upholstery, and only 100 or 150 for other smaller orders. Using customized rolls was common practice in the industry, but basic, uncustomized rolls in junkyards were not so easy to come by. Finding useful parts became quite an obsession of mine, for years I never missed an auction or shop closing. Who knows what you might find?

As the months ran into late summer we tried to anticipate issues as the machine took shape. Roger began to work full time in September, while I kept on with my sales work. We agreed that

Model of FLEXcon's first laminating machine with 35-year employee names etched in glass, 2016

I would split my salary with him equally. After all we were full partners. We had each invested $10,000 by the time we opened. Roger had no income at all, so it seemed fair to me to live on less until we started showing a profit.

We were ready to go by November. Through Roger, we were able to get the DuPont work, doing essentially the same thing Multi-Color had done for them. A big advantage for us was that DuPont had supplied the adhesives free of charge to Multi-Color to coat it onto the metalized Mylar® supplied by National Research. They supplied the adhesives to us as well, but don't think DuPont was being generous; they just wanted to protect their own formulas. All we had to do was run the machine and coat the metalized Mylar®, no material cost or inventory.

We were not solvent yet, but speaking of solvent, we didn't have enough money to buy any.

Often Alan Dragone, our National Research man, would come in around six with an order, and then come back at 1:00 a.m. to pick it up and drive all night to Newburgh, New York to have it there for the next workday. Roger and I would finish his order and be pulling the sticky Mylar® goo off of our hands—without solvent—at 1:00 a.m. to go home. We didn't mind though. There was not much business then anyway, just the two of us, but we were in business and about to go after the shoe trade in Boston.

One inevitable result of our work in that second story garage: it smelled, stunk, rather. No way around it. Coating stinks. Worse than rotting fruit or strong shoe polish. No way to cover it in those days. Here we were surrounded by houses, right across the street from a church. Our neighbors didn't much like us, not because of the trucks we brought in for delivery, but the smell which went right up the flue. People would bitch in the neighborhood. I'd go into the restaurant around the corner at 6:00 a.m. for coffee and the regulars would be talking about the young kid stinking up the neighborhood with his plastics. I'd be sitting right next to them at the counter and they would rattle on in French about me. They'd never seen me, didn't know I understood everything they said (the monastery had been run by French brothers after all), but I never let on that I understood. In a small town it's best to say nothing. The important thing was that we were on our way now. We were officially entrepreneurs.

A special note on becoming an entrepreneur: I had an opportunity to reflect on my entrepreneurship and speak to a class at WPI recently and I think I may have pissed the students off. I told the class that if you're born with a silver spoon in your mouth, there is no friggin' way you can make it as an entrepreneur. I saw a lot of frowns at that statement, but you have to be hungry—hungry enough to forget about weekends. They can't exist, nor can golf, tennis and vacations. To start a company, you have to commit yourself totally. You don't see your kids much. It's the price of commitment to the goal of making the company succeed during the critical formative years. If you're not willing to work the hundred-hour weeks, if you're not willing to be in the plant, cleaning the machines, on beautiful fall Sunday afternoons, when you'd rather be outside throwing a football to your sons, you don't stand much of a chance.

Having said that, you have to know, I embraced the idea of becoming an entrepreneur entirely. Making money drove the whole thing, of course. You don't grow up a poor kid from Ireland and go into business just to show how smart you are. At FLEXcon's 50th Anniversary celebration in 2006, I said, "The reason you start a business is money. What makes you happy though, are all the things you do—the development of new products, the selling, the interactions with all the people and places, but if the money's not there, it's not worth being around." Easy for me to say, fifty years after the decision to start the business, but what I said to that group, and to the WPI class, says a lot about my attitude back then, the only attitude you can have, as far as I can see, to start and sustain a business.

Myles breaking ground for FLEXcon's second plant, c. 1969

3

FLEXCON BEGINS

Soon I was on Beach Street, the center of shoe distribution in Boston, and once again our timing was right. Shoe manufacturers were looking for new ways to use vinyl coating and I was their man. I'd go into a place in the morning, get a sample and later match it to Mylar® and satisfy the customer. The shoe guys on Beach Street, South Street, and Kneeland Street thought they had exclusives with me, but little did they know I served them all. Of course, I could never eat lunch with any of them at the deli they all went to, for fear that another "exclusive" customer might see us. I couldn't show them our place in Spencer either. I had to tell them we were working on a secret Navy contract and to get in our plant they'd have to have secret clearance, so they could not come and see that half our orders were for their next-door competitors.

Roger and I were beginning to make some money finally. The shoe customers would supply the vinyl coated fabric and the metalized Mylar®. All we had to do was coat it, or sometimes we'd

coat and laminate it and be paid for both processes. Even better
when we'd coat, laminate and emboss, we got paid three times
for one go-around. In addition we were able to custom cut rolls
of 36- and 54-inch wide Mylar® with our slitter, an adjustable
razor blade, which we attached to our machine and measured
very precisely. We'd sell the custom cut rolls to our distributors
in Boston, who sold it in smaller amounts to individual shoemakers. We were also taking small orders for piping on upholstery,
but those orders were quickly growing. All of which was crowding us out of our upstairs garage on Maple Street.

By the end of 1958 the shoe business was going so well that
the garage was no longer big enough for our work. Roger and I
found the property of a former lumber company, the E. E. Stone
Company, that made boxes, located on the corner of nearby
Cherry and Wall Street, a deserted industrial area at the time.
We decided to buy it, and got a mortgage from Worcester County
National Bank for $26,000. In the process we signed our wives
and kids away. Mortgaging would become part of FLEXcon's
operating procedures in the future. Whenever we bought new
buildings we always mortgaged them, and eventually paid them
off. The shoebox approach of paying cash applied to equipment
and supplies only. Used equipment never makes money, but you
can always sell your building, and usually at a profit, so it was
worth the investment. It was a large brick building with two
floors and many doors for deliveries. One of my first decisions
was to declare our address on Wall Street, rather than Cherry, a
very recognizable mailing address. We had increased from 1,600
square feet on Maple Street, to 10,000 on Wall Street. Now we

just had to move our machine. Picture this:

> Two young men in sweaters and scarves slide a wooden pallet onto the hard-packed snow of the street. They are smiling and laughing, happy to be in the cold crisp sunshine, enjoying this strategy they have come up with to move the machine they have made, the center of their business, to a new and bigger location. The snow is slippery enough to allow them to pull a wooden pallet, with pieces of the machine on it, with ropes, as if it were a sled holding their children. When one slips and falls, the other's loud laugh rises in the cold still air. They pull the pallet up Church Street, then downhill on Mechanic, their breaths clouding the air, their shouts giddy as if they were kids on a snow day. Now a left onto Cherry and the goal, their new building at the corner, is within reach.

> People walking by stare at this creative maneuver, two men sliding a wooden pallet carrying a strange-looking frame with large rolls on a city street. Cars with chains pass slowly by. The two young men are buoyant with victory as they near their new building, their new place of business. They will set up their machine, their rolls, their chemicals and plastics. They will have more customers, more employees, and much more work here, but for now, they have a moment of unexpected fun in the blue-sky sunshine of a clean white world. They slide the pallet to one of the garage doors and it opens to receive it, while the two young men go back to slide another piece to its new home.

We were now located across the street from the railroad station, complete with a locomotive turn-around, and eventually a home for the elderly was built nearby. All of the residents could smell the same stink our former neighbors had loved so much. One old man who lived not far from our plant complained about

Wall Street building, c. 1976

the smell and so we bought him an air conditioner to clean out the air in his house. Pretty soon the word spread and I was providing air conditioners for all of the houses close enough to know about our pungent presence.

Now that we had more space, we had to buy more equipment. Sometimes it was expensive, or seemed so to us, and sometimes it didn't cost much at all—if you knew where to look. One of the inexpensive treasures I found were Bendix TM washing machine motors, which we used to power the rewind roll and make sure it was smooth and tight. We used a sewing machine pedal to control the speed, "wash" for slow or "spin dry" to speed up the rewind. As business picked up, the one part of our machine that would constantly wear out was the Bendix TM motors. Not a problem though, not if you knew where to get them at five bucks apiece. I would buy them cheap from a blind man named Oscar. He lived in the hills near Worcester and collected old appliances.

He made his money selling them to dealers who bought them for the sheet metal.

Oscar lived by himself, not even a junkyard dog to keep him company. He was in his fifties, I'd say, and pleasant enough. After my first couple of visits he knew my voice. He'd send me out back, and I'd root around for a while and come back with four or five Bendix TM motors. I'd put them on the table and he'd examine them with his hands, pronounce them as good. I'd pay him and I'd be off.

To keep the myth alive that I was strictly a white collar salesman-owner, we installed a buzzer and a peephole in the front door of the new location. I would go out in the morning to make calls and then come back and be part of our small work force because we needed all hands involved in producing new material and keeping the machines going. If a customer buzzed the front door, I'd take off for my office where I kept a suit, shirt and tie. By the time the customer made it to the office I was sitting behind my desk, suitably costumed and busy with paperwork.

As the business grew, Roger became less enthusiastic. He had too few jollities as the inside guy, the one in charge of production. I had my fun interacting with people, getting the work, being complimented, but Roger needed more. He liked to call himself the president of the company, but I didn't care if he called himself Jesus Christ as long as we were doing well, and we were. I remember when we made our first $25,000 each, he thought that was fine. As long as he was respected he felt fine. His ego was bigger than his pocket. My pocket was always bigger than my ego. That $25,000 was just the beginning for me. I probably should have recognized the warning signs then.

By 1959, Jean and I needed a break. I had become cranky and Jean was overwhelmed with kid-care. We hadn't had time off for a couple of years. A neighbor who knew someone in the Holland Cruise Lines suggested we take a two-week cruise. Before we left Roger wouldn't really talk to me and seemed annoyed that we were going. By the time we came back, I guess he'd made up his mind. "One of us has to buy the other out," he announced to me. I didn't argue, just asked his price.

I had always felt Roger would conk out. He didn't like the way the shoe business was going. He believed we'd go under, so I thought, if he wants out, I'll pay him off, half of the worth of the business' $250,000 in sales. I knew I wasn't going anywhere; I was elated to be the sole owner. Frankly, I didn't need Roger any more. I did at one point, but by then I had a willing, hard working crew of three. I knew I could get my $125,000 back. My friends, men I had helped set up in business, offered to buy in if I needed cash, but I didn't want anyone else in on my business.

Although $125,000 was a big amount in those days, especially at my young age with two small kids, I paid him pretty quickly. I started out by giving him $50,000 right away and then the other $75,000 over the next year. My lawyer got him to sign a non-compete agreement and we were done. Roger's last comment after the papers were signed: "I think I made a mistake getting out." Jean and I scraped along on mac and cheese for a while after that, but we made it through because we had to. When I go back and think about how I managed it, I wonder what the Christ I was doing.

*Myles standing on loading dock of Plant I on Wall Street,
Spencer, Massachusetts, c. 1965*

Roger and I got along fine; there was never any arguing. My only concern was that Roger could never accept responsibility for any flawed orders. If there was a mistake he always had to be right, the customer must have given the wrong specs. I, on the other hand, always wanted to get the bad taste out of a customer's mouth as quickly as possible; replace the order at no cost, we could make up the profit loss in future orders. I saw no point in fighting with the customer, why create a negative relationship? Roger did not agree. Overall our partnership had been good though. It was just time. The net result was that I became the sole proprietor of FLEXcon, the name I had always wanted for the corporation. When we first started Roger had wanted to call us Custom Coating and Laminating, to explain exactly what we were doing. I'm glad I didn't go along though; FLEXcon was much more appropriate, combining the words flexible and converter, considering the wide ranging future direction of the company. Converting, applied to our business, means to bring two plastic films together to convert, or develop, them into a product that is both usable and attractive for consumer products. We search for creative ways to combine materials, producing the least expensive and most effective products we can.

A couple of years later Roger opened his own business and named it, of course, Custom Coating and Laminating. He was able to fund his building with the money (from the settlement) and started off well. Ironically, I became one of his biggest customers. He violated our non-compete agreement, but I did not go after him legally. The financial and time commitment of legal action just wasn't worth it. Besides, I was able to make a lot of money from adhesive coating some of his matte materials. I didn't have the time to develop my own matte topcoats then and I knew where to get rid of the materials he made, so I never mentioned the contract. It's always better to seize opportunity than to waste time in negative action. By the 80s I was buying about $9 million worth of raw materials a year from him. When he later decided to sell his business, my numbers helped boost up his selling price to $25 million.

At the same time Roger inadvertently sent business my way. One of his customers, Art Summers from Tadco Manufacturing, once asked, "Why do I need you when I've got Roger?"

"I can't answer that question," I said, "Roger's a good guy, stick with him. I'll tell you one thing, I'll be around when you get your first refusal of credit." Sure enough, Roger wouldn't take back a flawed batch from Art for credit towards a new order. The phone rang a few days later and I had Art from that point on.

By the way, one last Roger note. Years later, in the 70s, when my FLEXcon guys and I toured Multi-Color to determine what we could buy as they were closing up shop, the Vice President of Manufacturing called me over to a dark corner of a storeroom. There, in the corner, was basically my machine! The very one Roger and I had put together from the design Roger created, same framing, and same type of rollers. This was where he had gotten the goddamn design. He had acted as if he created the whole thing and there it was at Multi-Color. No wonder our first machine was so good!

In 1961, I got into a whole new world of dyeing the Mylar® to create gold. It was almost like medieval alchemy. I could take

Gold lamé shoes, c. 1960

laminated yellow and orange metalized Mylar® and make it look like 18 or 24 carat gold lamé, a very popular material for women's shoes and handbags. Here's how it happened. National Research wanted out of the metalizing business in 1959. So, we were able to buy their left-over metalized Mylar® by the pound, instead of the yard, at a very good price—it came out to four cents a yard rather than twenty-five. Alan Dragone (who subsequently left National Research for the Celenese Corporation) had a lot of 40-inch wide roll stuff hanging around and I needed 36-inch. More importantly for us though, they metalized against a drum, in effect using only one side, which was for our purposes of dyeing, perfect, because it did not allow dust to that side. I held onto the stuff for a while and then it became very useful. We looked up the patents for making Dacron thread, but instead of thread, we wanted to dye film. Norman Collette, who had taken over the position as main inside man after Roger left in January, 1960, and I changed machine #1 to a dyeing machine. Machine #2 prepared the Mylar® and did the laminating and embossing. We developed a new dyeing process we called sublimation. We were already coating the Mylar® as if we were printing. Now the big questions: how do we print a dye? Not only print it, but make it uniform? Especially when we put the dye in a solution as thin as water which will drip off and streak the roll, ruining the uniform application?

We worked it out so that the dye would stay on the film uniformly, but then we had to get rid of the solution, and we had to get rid of it by drying the solution from the dye before the roll of film passed the first idler, the cylinder that takes the roll to the next process. Otherwise as the roll turns on the cylinder, the wet dye would streak and screw up the whole batch. How to dry it though? Jean graciously sacrificed one of our wedding gifts, a fan, to do the trick. The fan would play on the roll as it went through to make sure the roll was dry. As soon as the liquid dried, it turned to powder, and then the roll would pass over a drum heated to 350 degrees heating the remaining particles of dye into the film in a uniform pattern. The film finally went around a cold cylinder to make sure it was flat again.

So, was I really an alchemist? I'd say yes, at least for making money for the company. The shoe guys loved the gold lame and I had over 3,000 yards of material to sell to them.

The story gets better. It could have gotten much worse though, at least for the shoemakers because as you know, women's fashions, particularly shoe fashions, change like the wind, or at least like a seasonal wind. What's hot in the spring may be gone by the fall, and will surely be gone by the next spring. So, what's a shoe guy to do with all the vinyl coated material he has left over, the stuff that sells for a buck a yard?

Come to Myles, that's what. The pinks and purples needed to have the PLA oil be stopped off or not allowed to migrate into the metalized Mylar®. So I created an adhesive coating to go on top of the Mylar® and then laminated it to the vinyl material. That became the base we needed and all those left over pink and purple rolls were back in the game. I was able to become an alchemist again and turn those rolls into silver or gold. To do this process, I was getting not a dollar a yard, the normal price, but two, and the reclaiming process only cost me twenty cents a yard to do. The shoe manufacturers had never heard of such a deal. They sold for four bucks the stuff that they could only have made a dollar a yard on, if that. I was able to turn their junk, literally, into gold for them!

By the way, this dyeing business was conducted under the name Myles Processing. Mylar® and Myles, close enough, so that some people thought I'd invented it, a product that had been in the U.S. since 1950.

As we became larger, the shoe people began to order in quantities of two thousand yards. That threw up a red flag to me. Orders of fifty, even a hundred yards were okay, but big orders were potentially trouble. I remember getting a big order from a New York slipper outfit on a Monday. They wanted the shipment to arrive at their place on a Friday afternoon, not on Friday morning, not on Monday. It had to be Friday afternoon. Not by coincidence, the slipper outfit went out of business that same Friday afternoon. Phones, offices, everything gone, including my big order. They'd have a brother-in-law or somebody put the order in a truck and deliver it to Lawrence or Lowell and you'd never find it or be able to trace it and I'd be out two to four thousand bucks.

In the 60s there was always a middleman you had to go through, and that's how things got lost. I could never trace a thing. Sometimes I'd walk into a shoe factory and see my stuff and know goddamn well I had never shipped it to them. I'd just have to let it go though.

Shoe distributors were losing out to direct ordering too. We still needed each other though, the shoe guys and me. They hung on as long as they could and I still serviced them, but I knew it was only a matter of time before I'd have to make a change, a big change, if FLEXcon was going to stay in business. I no longer wanted to take materials from people and coat it with Mylar®, having to take the chance that two or three thousand yard orders would get "lost" somehow. I needed to attract more sophisticated, bigger, companies and to do that I'd have to change directions, in many ways start a new business. Since my time at Johnson & Johnson, working with technical tapes and adhesives, I had kept it in my mind that pressure-sensitive was the way to go. It was time to act on that idea.

Opening of the FLEXcon Tech Center, 2012

4

INNOVATIONS

I BELIEVED AT the time and I believe today that the most important decision I ever made was spending $60,000 to buy a machine that changed the direction of FLEXcon. The head of quality control at Permacel knew when different machines came on the market, and he also knew that I was interested in pressure-sensitive. He told me about an available machine in Rhode Island at the Arkwright Finishing Company which made matte coating on 3- and 5-millimeter Mylar® to make plastic graph paper for draftsmen. The matte coating had to be perfectly smooth and thick—.008 and .010 mil so that permanent drafting copies could be made on 1 mil of matte coating. Lucky for us the machine did not behave as it should have for Arkwright. It was very sophisticated with a main motor connected by chains to a series of small motors with different speeds, which were supposed to provide the perfectly smooth coating needed for the smooth graph work. However, the machine did not cooperate; it did a kind of jog, which did not give continuity to coating.

The people at Arkwright couldn't correct the problem, maybe that's why they sold this brand new $115,000 machine to me for $60,000. Arkwright then ordered a new and even more sophisticated machine from Black Clawson—a major manufacturer of coating machines in the U.S. for $250,000.

When I bought the machine from Arkwright, I didn't even know anything was wrong with it. Once I realized it, I experimented a bit, took the small motors out of the picture and made all processes go through the main motor. The result: no more jog at least not enough to bother the pressure-sensitive work because the coating covered up flaws. I have no idea why this big company couldn't figure out the problem.

Buying this machine took FLEXcon in an entirely new direction. None of my competitors in the laminating business ever would have spent $60,000 for such a machine, mainly because they didn't know what the hell pressure-sensitive was all about. An easy way to think of the pressure-sensitive concept is to think of masking tape or electrical tape. In both cases the material is coated with an adhesive, which when you press on it, sticks. It is sensitive to the pressure applied. Working at Johnson & Johnson developing pressure-sensitive materials, gave me critical insight into the potential of my new direction, but I should also add that my decision to go into adhesive coated Mylar® and vinyl using a release liner instead of a tape negated any idea of being in competition with my former employers.

Fasson, Morgan, and 3M, the big names in the pressure-sensitive industry were all working with paper, in other words transferring or pressing the paper to the released liner for labels.

Paper was easy to work with because these companies could make long runs on the machine quickly. The paper lay straight and flat with no gauge bands, offering a smooth surface, which made the process error-free, and profitable. When Fasson or Morgan bought the metalized Mylar® laminate from McCord, they had to buy it in minimum orders of 1,500 yards or 2,000 yards of 56-inch width. These big companies would charge up to $6 a yard to apply pressure-sensitive to the metalized Mylar® they bought for $2, a very healthy profit. They'd run the whole 1,500 yards through their machines because they coated the release liner on one end with silicone and laminated the pressure sensitive liner to the laminate in the middle. However, most customers of pressure-sensitive didn't need 1,500 yards of the same embossed material. If a customer wanted 300 yards of laminated embossed metalized Mylar®, the company had the rest hanging around, already embossed. All dressed up with nowhere to go.

I figured out a radically different way. In fact, I was in competition with McCord because I made the laminates myself. Since I did the laminating at FLEXcon, I could coat all 1,500 yards and, because I already had a number of customers, I knew I could get rid of the 1,500 yards in small increments putting in the embossing after the pressure sensitive. I'd wait until I had a specific order to emboss. If you wanted to emboss a hundred yards, I had no problem. McCord's would only take 1,500 yard minimum and they'd satisfy the order in three weeks—if you were lucky. If you came to me and told me Fasson's or Morgan's price, I'd give you 10% off, and I'd have your embossed hundred yards for you in three days. This was a new way of doing business. We became the leading pressure-sensitive company in metalized Mylar® because we could do everything in-house and fast.

In laminating, there were a lot of guys on the block, crowding up the competition. Now I was the only kid on the block, the only one who had a handle on this new pressure sensitive material. I had learned a lot about business already, and in this second shot at starting a business, I knew I had to make customer service the most important priority. I know a lot of companies will make the same claim, but I wanted to put FLEXcon to the test. First, I'd try to accommodate any customer's request, taking on all those smaller accounts that the big companies ignored. Second, I'd adopted the dry cleaner's philosophy: in by ten, out by five. Okay, so same day could never actually happen, but the philosophy, the attitude of fast delivery, was to become a hallmark of FLEXcon. Even with the larger orders, we would eventually begin to get, I kept that philosophy. Again, we blew away the competition. We had the plant set up for doing every aspect of the order at one location. We could coat, pressure-sensitive, laminate, and emboss, all under one roof.

Some of this success was luck. It may have been good timing and it was definitely good planning. First the machine I needed to do the pressure-sensitive work, then the strategy to accommodate smaller orders, then the commitment to get those orders out fast. I saw the niche, the need, and our business grew.

By 1962, I had Norman Collette, Allen Fontaine, and Tom Jacques, my top three guys, along with Phil Rhault and Bob Gagne working for me, with me really, and they worked hard. Incidentally, Tom came to us when he was 19. He was my wife's

Myles with Allen Fontaine, one of his first team members, 2006

nephew and I put him through college. Tom, like the others I mentioned, stayed with us for over forty years. What motivated the people who worked for FLEXcon? Simple. When I made money, I gave money. That's always been my thinking. Our people have always been well paid, more then they'd make anywhere else. It was always worth it to me.

When I later had salesmen on commission, I paid 5%, 7%, sometimes even 10% when most other salespeople were getting 2%. Some guys would sell to get their averages—the 5% salesmen, but some guys like Brad Barber only shot for 10%. He'd concentrate on high profit products and he'd do it well. If guys like him were getting 10% imagine what the Christ I was getting, and I was happy to pay it!

Don't get the wrong impression. The money wasn't always easy. Once, in the early 60s, I found out on a Wednesday that I couldn't make payroll on Friday. We had paid out a lot that week and for some reason accounts receivable had not caught up. I was $700 short. Can you imagine the impact of McDonough not meeting his Friday payday!

I put on my suit and went up to the bank to meet the bank manager, who in his most polite and patient manner told me he could not give me a loan. Bank policy was that a committee had to meet before corporate loans could be given, and that committee wouldn't meet until Tuesday. All the way back to the plant I anxiously imagined the rumors that would spread in small town Spencer. Everyone would think I had bitten off too much. Word would get out and orders would slow to a trickle, all because of $700.

Then at noon, Phil Rhault went to the bank to borrow $500 to help pay for a motorcycle. Twenty minutes later he returned, check in hand. I was furious. He couldn't pay the friggin' loan unless I had a loan, the stupid bastards! So I went back to the manager and said, "Let's cut the shit, will ya? I don't normally speak this way, (at least not to bank mangers I'm trying to get a loan from) but I need this money! You just lent $500 to one of my employees. If I can't pay him, how can he pay you?"

The bank manager tried to smile, but his face wouldn't let him. Instead he excused himself, went to a desk and spoke quietly into the phone. I got my loan. I had to repay in two weeks, which I

Some of the original team members (from left) *Tom Jacques, Myles,*
Allen Fontaine and Dave Ingalls, c. 2000

did, after I called a few customers to pay their bills. A momen-
tary problem, a potentially critical one for me and the company,
a problem Phil or anybody else never knew about as he drove
around on that motorcycle.

A crucial ingredient of FLEXcon's success has been innovation. Remember Corfam shoes and the "wet look" of women's
coats in the early 60s? They became big money makers for
FLEXcon. DuPont made Corfam artificial leather for shoes, but
they did not want to get into colors. Phillip Premier, a distribu-
tor for DuPont-Newburgh which brought DuPont into the shoe
trade, convinced them that women wanted more colors in shoes

than the black and white offered though. A shoe guy I knew in Boston recommended me. Sure I said, no problem, we can do that. I always had a "we-can-do-that" attitude, but, to be honest, I didn't always know if we could do it. We always said we could and then tried to figure it out after.

DuPont presented us with just such a situation. There was a problem, a big problem, or I should say, a very small one, 0.8 millimeters to be exact. That's the thickness of the urethane casting we had to apply to keep the color accurate. That's a little less than a thousandth of an inch. At 0.9 you had a different color, at 0.7 it was closer, but at 0.8 the leather had the color and could "breathe." We got the urethane from AJ Quinn of Malden, Massachusetts, and their chemist, Al DeNuzio. We experimented, fooled around with it, finally used only 7% solids of the solution, sending 93% up the flue, which you can no longer do because of pollution laws (now everybody has to use at least 50% of the solids of solution) and gave Phillip Premier and DuPont their accurate colors.

Now that I could do the colors for shoes, another industry wanted me to do colors for "wet" look materials for woman's fashions. I was able to make a coating for the fabric, which had polyurethane foam on it, by melting the foam a bit with heat, then laminating it with polyurethane film which attached itself to the foam, and there you'd have it: the melted polyurethane foam with polyurethane film—a shiny material that looked like it just came out of the rain.

The word spread that I was the guy who started the wet look business. I was getting 5,000 and 10,000 yard orders. FLEXcon was humming; profits were up. We were quickly expanding, doubled the work force, and doubled the profit. Then I received an order for 100,000 yards of black "wet" material from Sears. I took the order, but told the Sears supplier it would be the last one I'd take from them. They'd have to go someplace else. I would have knocked myself out of the pressure-sensitive business if I had stayed with orders that big. I knew I was making a lot of money, but I also knew I could be stuck. Women's fashions change too easily, they were not going to be the focus of FLEXcon. Sears was pissed, so I set them up with Plastic Film Corp. a vinyl fabric business. Plastic Film developed waterproof laminates for the Army, and I had sold them adhesives back when I worked for Rubber and Asbestos. I knew Plastic Film could handle the orders and they made Sears happy.

In 1962 automobile manufacturers used flocked Mylar® to keep car windows in place. Their suppliers flocked the fabric of five millimeter thick Mylar® into a plush, that was then inserted into the window channels to provide a cushioned support on both sides of the window. There was one problem—in the desert heat of the southwest the Mylar® shrank and fell out of the channels, no longer providing support. Jo-Ann Fabrics of Lowell, Massachusetts, a supplier to Standard Insulation, came to me for help.

The next day I had a solution. I ran the Mylar® around a Teflon® drum heated to 375 degrees and shrank it down before it was flocked, then embossed it flat to its original condition. They only had to flock the Mylar® on one side of each channel, the side up against the window. I reversed the shrink process and bingo, because the Mylar® was already shrunk, it worked. It did not fall out of the channel in hot climates anymore.

This was the first time, by the way, that I, or anyone else for that matter, had experimented with making Mylar® non-shrinkable at high temperatures. Did I try to protect my new idea with a patent though? No. FLEXcon's name was already known as a company that will try many approaches, that's how we grew. People with problems would come to us and see what we could do. Our solution often ended up in new ideas and new products. Printed circuits made with pre-shrunk Mylar® laminated to copper eventually became a big item. When the volume got large, DuPont could handle it because they had the big machines that could shrink the Mylar® in long ovens and then emboss on a cold roll which flattens it out again, all in one long flow. So, sometimes when volume got large we'd lose to the biggies.

Another example is release-coating. At first only small companies made the released coated Mylar®. In fact, Roger's Custom Coating was the first. Then DuPont saw an opportunity. All they had to do was put on a gravure coating, keep it going, put the silicone on and they started to sell release-coated Mylar® in large quantities. FLEXcon bought $5,000 worth in the beginning. Now we spend over $25 million a year with DuPont. For FLEXcon, the Mylar® film is far superior to paper. Paper release liner, for example, will sometimes give a mottled look, whereas release film will always be smooth. Did you ever notice what happened to the paper label of your shampoo bottle when it got wet in the shower? It peeled off. Not so with film, it's a permanent label. It resists the hot water and soap.

To get back to patents, ideas, such as mine, start out as embryos, but when they become big, someone else takes it over. I did not do patents because the big companies were going to take the ideas anyway. You just keep your mouth shut and move on. After all, the 4,000 yard orders were nothing to the big companies, but we got good money for them and it was easy to do: just heat up the drum more than it would be at one end and flatten it out at the end with the cold drum to shrink the Mylar® before the final product or use. Patenting was not on my mind.

Early testing of the front cones of U.S. spacecrafts demonstrated that on re-entry into the earth's atmosphere they would burn up because of extreme heat. This became a major impediment to space exploration in manned and unmanned spacecrafts. The problem of how to prevent them from burning up was given to my good friend Dick Silverman of HySil Corporation—the leading metalizer in the country at that point. Metalized material was necessary to ward off the heat; however, there was another problem. In order to develop insulation to keep the heat at a manageable level inside the spacecraft there had to be pockets of air in the material. Dick approached me to help him develop effective insulation. We knew that the material had to be a certain thickness and it had to be crinkled to be effective as a heat shield. I tried working with Mylar® in the beginning, but soon changed to Kapton®, the only high temperature plastic around. The material for the insulation had to be flexible, therefore no thermoset products would do. Also, and just as important, Kapton® could withstand temperatures up to 600 degrees whereas Mylar® could only handle up to 400 degrees.

I made a very deep embossing and when the material came out of the machine I was able to crimp the material even more. I used Kapton®, metallization, air, and then Kapton® again. If you emboss either Mylar® or Kapton® there's a pocket of air between the metalized surfaces. If you have deep penetration of embossing and roll it slowly, the pocket becomes thicker with air and those pockets of air between the layers provide the insulation. What started as a roll six inches in diameter inflated to thirty-six inches with the air pockets. We had to pay close attention to the process, four guys slowly doing each roll, and we had to wear white gloves so moisture wouldn't interfere with the metalizing. You could liken the result to the pocket of air between two panes of glass in today's windows, but our insulation had to be flexible, which made it impossible to determine the exact thickness of the air pocket.

I preserved the crinkle by rolling the Kapton® in a very different way (trade secret). Kapton®, metalized, and embossed by FLEXcon, became the answer to insulation on nose cones of spacecrafts. That insulation protection has been used in every spacecraft that's gone up from the beginning.

I got a fortune for that work and Dick did, too. It seems that the more expensive the raw material, $50 a pound for Kapton®, the more money you make. When you have to pay that much for something, you know it's important, in this case enough so to protect the lives of space explorers and their crafts. The fun, the excitement that kept me working all those long hours in this business was just this: bringing in new products in ways we never even thought of earlier.

Dick Silverman, c. 1982
Photo by Bacharach

Although this product was extremely successful, I told Dick I
did not want my name associated with it. He did all the metalizing in his plant and all the negotiating, so he was able to get
all the contracts, and I wanted him to get all the credit. Besides,
if word got out about what I did for him, all the other metalizers
would have been after me to do similar work for them. It would
have been difficult for me to refuse them. At the time, I was selling all the other metalizers dyed Mylar®, which they metalized
the color gold for their customers. If I did refuse their requests to
do work like Dick's they might have switched to the only other

guy who dyed Mylar®. On the other hand, if I had taken on more work like this, I would have been too busy and lost all the dyeing business to my competitor anyway. Better in this case to keep my mouth shut.

In those days if you could keep your doors open—merely stay in business—there was so much innovation coming along you almost had to make it. Just keep the doors open and something would come along.

One such opportunity was Speidel, the watchmakers. They came to me because the Japanese had developed a bracelet watchband in gold and sold it for ninety-nine cents. Speidel could have made a similar one for far less with my dyed Mylar®, but at first decided against it because they didn't want to undercut their own watchband sales. Speidel had never used Mylar® in their metal bands, but a year later Dick Carter, their development man, came to me looking for a way to laminate plastic to metal, simulating leather.

Mylar® cannot be "coined," or made to hold a design that can be repeated. It has a memory as we say—it reverts back to its original form. I had to come up with a way to combine Mylar®, which was, after all, an inexpensive material, with another material that could do the job, a familiar challenge, the very essence of the term "converter." So, I made up a Mylar®-Tedlar® combination. The Mylar® held to the metal and the Tedlar® on top had the ability to coin. Tedlar®, often used in wall covering, is a polyvinyl fluoride film, which can be embossed. Putting the Tedlar® on top of the Mylar® allowed the plastic to be imprinted in a similar fashion. What Speidel did before on metal, they could now coin in black or brown imitation leather laminated to their metal base.

There was one problem though; human perspiration proved to break down the adhesive in the watchbands. The new adhesive formula demanded a large amount of toxic solvents and cross-linking ingredients for the 56-inch wide plastic laminate, cut to fit Speidel's specs.

So I had to go to Speidel and tell them we could not do this work because my people were getting sick from the chemicals. Rather than keeping the customer and putting my employees at risk, I decided to help develop a new machine at Speidel that could make the material for the watchbands in two-inch wide sections. The machine would be of little use to FLEXcon, but significantly cut down on the amount of toxins and made it safer for them to run. I gave Speidel the formulas and let them do all the work and keep the profit themselves.

The project was not fruitless for FLEXcon though. We put ourselves in a whole new business by taking plastic and making it look like leather. We were always interested in expanding our business and the fact that we were a young company helped us out too.

Sometimes guys can take over a family business and they will keep it going as it has always gone before. If they expand by doing more of the same they consider themselves successful. As a new business we had to be flexible though and go after new products. If we could find new ways to help other businesses grow, then we could grow ourselves—an important aspect of FLEXcon's success. I realized that if I was innovative and my product helped the customer make more money I could charge as much as I wanted. I usually knew his prices, what he was going to make, and charged accordingly.

In 1964 I stumbled upon a great idea about how to give metalized Mylar® a new use: a brushed stainless steel finish. The way we got into brushing is kind of crazy. A 2 millimeter Mylar® pressure-sensitive shipment was returned because it had scratches. I realized it must have dragged over the idler when it was sheeted or slit. What would happen, I wondered, if we figured out a way to really put some scratches into it? Phil Rhault, Norman Collette, and I spent about six months trying to figure it out. Finally, we found that if we scratched the clear Mylar® by sanding it, and then metalized it on the scratched side we could see the scratched, or brushed, side underneath. Then we put the pressure-sensitive on the metalized side creating a brushed see-through stainless steel look.

One of the great advantages of this new product had to do with camber. Once stainless steel is disturbed or bent, it stays that way. My brushed pressure-sensitive product gave the look of ordinary stainless steel, but was far less expensive and if disturbed it could come back to its original shape. It didn't take long to sell it to companies like GE for clock facings, refrigerators, washing machines, or for Whirlpool and Bendix TM nameplates. The market for brushed stainless steel really took off after that. Other companies had developed embossed vinyl plastic with a similar look, but when it was heated it lost its abraded affect. It took them eight years to figure out what I was doing. Too late!

By the way, our business was, and still is, full of espionage—

spy stuff. A lot of people thought we invented something tricky with this Mylar®. If other companies could find out how we did the brushed stainless steel, I'm sure they'd sell a few of their grandmothers for the information. I was so secure with my people and the company was small enough that I never even worried about patents. I told my guys that if you let someone into FLEXcon, there goes your overtime, maybe even your job. So they were always on the alert for snoopers—truck drivers were the worst. Sometimes they'd come in for a shipment and kind of hang around waiting for the load to be completed, eyes darting all over the place. They would take a stroll around if they could, maybe just curious, but sometimes a new employee of another company, maybe a chemist or someone familiar with the production, was sent in as a truck driver, to see if he could pick up on any clues. I was really sanding, not brushing, and if someone saw the upstairs, he'd pick up a lot. If we caught a spy, and we sometimes did, we'd get rid of the guy, get him out of there fast. We were doing so much new stuff and there was so much going on, we could have had major problems if the competition used our techniques. Legal action wasn't worth the trouble. You couldn't accuse anyone unless you knew for sure, and the legal costs would be impossible, but the attempts at spying were a good indication that we were headed in the right direction.

The pressure-sensitive market changed the company dramatically. No longer were we doing things for ten or twenty-five cents. The more expensive the raw material the better the mark-up and profit. If customer can take your material and double their price—that's it!

In the 60s I was DuPont's fair-haired kid on Mylar®. Whenever they had a customer with a Mylar® problem they sent him to me. I ended up meeting a lot of DuPont's European customers this way. The word from the U.S. was that this kid (I was only in my early thirties then) was really good on these new ideas for converting Mylar® into usable products for different trades. These new connections made me hopeful that FLEXcon could be successful in the European market.

The DuPont people had set me up with potential customers, but I was truly on my own. I knew nothing about the cities, the languages, or the people of Europe. I ended up coming up with a pretty brilliant time-saving idea though. As soon as I landed in a new country I would find a taxi driver who spoke English. That night I'd take him out to dinner and hire him for the next day, for double, maybe triple, his usual fee. In the morning I would give him a brief training on one or two of my products. He knew the city and how to find the customers I'd made appointments with. He would go into the office of a potential customer, where he'd relay the knowledge he knew of my products. If the customer wanted to know more, I'd go in. If the taxi driver was not successful, I'd stay in the car and we'd move on to the next one.

Although I was the first one over there with new ideas for the various uses of Mylar® I had problems even giving out samples. I found out that Europeans did not like to do business with American suppliers. Too many American companies had gone to Europe and if they didn't make it in two years they pulled out, leaving only a representative in a rented office. The potential European customers were especially cautious because of the time—it took three weeks, not including the production—and cost of shipping. So I had a lot of convincing to do. I'd go to these European cities and try to persuade customers that, not only did this new plastic have great potential, but also that I would be there for a long time and could provide quick service. I was stubborn. I wanted to stay with it. Call it ego, or maybe because I was so young, I was inexperienced enough to look for markets in other countries before I had gone very far into my own. I thought I could make easy sales because I had something new. It took a lot of visits, two weeks at a time, every five or six months, before anything happened. I would stumble around in a fog of jet-lag; sometimes I would be on a train and sleep right through my stop. I must admit I never really enjoyed the travel. It became just another phase of growing the business. We started out getting some small orders, but it took a good five years to get them to realize I was there for the long haul, and another twenty-five before FLEXcon built a plant in Europe.

Myles at FLEXcon, 1977

5

CONNECTIONS

AN ENTREPRENEUR KNOWS that his company can be successful if his sense of loyalty and trust are directed at the people working for him. His employees have to feel the same sense of job security he does. He must also develop a level of cooperation, so that if a mistake is made that same mistake will not be repeated. If things go wrong or someone does not have the proper attitude his people must feel free to tell his management, who will find a way to fix the problem or weed out the individual. The entrepreneur strengthens loyalty chiefly through his personality. He cannot demand it. He must show concern for his employees through his personal attention so that they know he is there to help them with any problems. He pays them well; he provides good health benefits; he shares.

Let's face it: without a hard-working, well-motivated, contented bunch working for you, you don't really stand much of a chance as an entrepreneur. People coming to work for FLEXcon knew they'd be paid well. They knew we had never laid anyone off. Tough times, yes, but in tough times I had people paint the interiors just to keep them on the payroll. I was loyal to them, and I also wanted a trained, capable staff ready to go when things got better.

One of the greatest sources of pride for me has been my employees. I have always tried to know each of them by name. I wanted to be able to go anywhere in the building and be greeted with a familiar smile. The men and women who worked for me have always been very important to me. I treated them well, not just because it produced good work, but because I wanted to. Perhaps it was that I grew up in a working class family, and worked hard myself, or maybe just because of an innate interest in people and their lives but, I have always had respect for them and the work they do. I want to focus on some of the people and the human intangibles in FLEXcon's history. Situations that do not show up on any bottom line but have an impact on the way the business moves forward.

I always rewarded the salespeople with meetings and vacations in places like Puerto Rico or Arizona. During one such meeting I gave them some advice, "I was a salesman myself, and I know how tough it is being away all week. When you go away your wife is in charge of the kids. Then you come back, you think you're in charge of them, and your wife thinks, 'That son of a bitch! He's gone all week and he thinks he's in charge?'" The salesmen laughed, but then I got serious. "This is how divorces start. I have an idea for you though. On a Friday night, while your wife puts the kids to bed, you get out the candles, spread out a blanket, some food, open a bottle of wine, and have a picnic

Myles with (left) *Mabel Guy and* (right) *Jeannette Byczek*
c. 1977

on the living room floor with her. If you ever wanted loving, you'll get it that night. Have that picnic every so often, so she knows you're thinking of her." By the next week, some of those guys started coming up to me with smiles on their faces. Living room picnic, hell of an idea!

An employee's family was always important to me. Whenever I interviewed a candidate for an executive position, I also interviewed his wife. Or I should say Jean and I interviewed the couple. Much became apparent in such an interview. Will the wife object to her husband's travel? Does she have a personality to be part of a team? How do the two seem to interact? Most of the men seeking these positions were talented, articulate candidates. Sometimes the couple interview could mean the difference in our decision making. Jean and I would sit down and discuss our reactions to the husband and wife.

My employees knew I took a special interest in their families. Sometimes they would even ask me to intervene if their child was not doing well in school or was in some kind of trouble. They hoped maybe I could scare them straight. Their kid would come into my office looking scared because he's in his father's boss's office. I'd tell the kid that I was there to be his friend though, and that I wanted to work with him on the problem. We would talk alone for forty-five minutes or so. I would always stress the importance of his education, learning a good trade, or maybe even working for us someday, but he had to show he could cooperate with school, and develop some discipline first. Usually the employee would come tell me a couple weeks later that their child was doing better. Sometimes I would even call the school principal and check up on the kid myself. When I was in a position to help fathers with their children, even though I might end up late for dinner with my own sons, I always thought I had to do it. It was important to me.

As FLEXcon's business expanded, we had to physically expand as well. In 1969 I took the big step, and risk, of buying thirty-five acres on South Spencer Road for about $35,000 from John Foley. One of John's hobbies was clearing land with his bulldozer, but he had only cleared about five acres at the time. I knew, even then, that I would need more in the future though, so I bought all thirty-five. I was worried that as FLEXcon grew more successful, the price on any surrounding land would rise accordingly. The thing about land is, if you have it you don't have to worry about getting it. I completed these land purchases long before the last building, the corporate office, was constructed in 1988. I knew early on that we would have to expand to keep achieving our goals.

Once I had bought the land I focused on the equipment I would fill it with. I bought a machine at an auction in New Jersey for $25,000. I went to every auction I could find in those days. I'd usually see the same guys at these auctions, doing the same thing I did, checking things out. Sometimes we'd get together on items rather than bid against each other. For example, I'd buy two machines at a lower price, and then sell one to the other guy who wanted it. We'd both save money. The one I bought for $25,000 was the first to go into the South Spencer Road property.

There was one catch. The new property was still just trees and fields. We would not be able to complete construction and move the new machine in for two years, so I decided to store it at our truck company's warehouse. It had to be taken apart first, before it was stored, but there was no construction manual available. We knew we would never be able to remember how to put it together again without some guidance. We needed a creative solution. So, we took hundreds of Polaroid photos as we broke it down. We were lucky we took those photos, because the machine turned out to be a work horse, lasting thirty-five years.

As a business expands and you have to hire more, you sometimes have to fire people. One of the first I had to fire set the

75

precedent for later terminations. As we expanded Plant I we had no place to put the machine I'd bought from Arkwright, so I leased a building owned by Monsanto in Bondsville, about forty minutes from FLEXcon. I put Gerry Collette in charge of the building and hired a quality control guy from Permacel to run the machine. The floor of the building was uneven which Monsanto fixed by pouring asphalt over it. It was easier, less expensive than trying to put new concrete over the old concrete, which would not bind anyway, or tearing up the whole floor. I was stupid enough to go along with the idea. I say stupid because three things happened as a result of the asphalt—all bad.

First, it was summer, and after about a month the asphalt got soft and the weight of the machine settled in at uneven angles, so that the material did not run through the machine properly. Second, the machine had run on steam at Arkwright, but we had to convert to gas to run it at Bondsville. The local gas company had problems with the conversion and the machine gave us surprises we never wanted. After about ten minutes of operation, it would explode—Bang! Bang! And we'd run out of the building, fearing for our lives. I'd fix the problem, get the thing running again, but the next day Gerry would always call me up again. It seems that the quality control guy would screw around with the motors of the machine after I left; undoing everything I had just done to fix them. We were using the machine to produce samples, which I desperately needed for my European sojourns. This guy was sabotaging my strategy! How could I convince a business in Genoa or Luxemburg that I could get a whole order to him in speedy fashion with this goddamn machine break-down?

Not only that—and this is the third bad thing—Gerry complained that the guy would sit around the office much of the day cleaning rifles he had brought in. We worried about this employee. Something was wrong there. He was distracted, not focused on work, and I had to get him out of there.

I called my lawyer, Maurice Ulin, told him I wanted to meet him and the employee at the Salem Cross Inn, a restaurant I frequented that had a private room where we could talk. I called my lawyer because I wanted a witness and for the employee to sign termination papers. I needed a mostly public place away from work. It is not that I feared he would have one of his guns with him, not much anyway; I just wanted a civilized way to terminate him. I came to use that restaurant, and that room, "the firing room," with my lawyer present, whenever I had to terminate an employee. It was unpleasant business at best, but often the only resolution to a difficult situation. Years later whenever we had to get rid of a disgruntled employee—in a large work force you sometimes have one or two—we always had a cop nearby, just in case. We made sure we moved the fired employee out of the building as quickly as possible, made sure he turned in his entry pass and made sure all the doors were locked. All this has always been done quietly, often without most other employees even knowing about it. Caution is always best.

In 1965, my three companies, FLEXcon, Myles Processing and Vari-Coating, merged and became simply FLEXcon, Inc. We were approaching the million dollar sales mark and I began to feel the pressure of keeping up with the research, experimentation, sales, and production. I wanted someone to help me, both in running the business and as a salesman. I had a pair of brothers, Norman and Gerry Collette running the manufacturing aspects, but I needed someone with chemistry and business experience for a fast growing FLEXcon. I approached a salesman from Tedlar at DuPont, named Mark Ungerer, with the chemistry background I was looking for. His interviews revealed that he had the experience and personality to fit my needs. I hired him as our general manager, in charge of the day-to-day running of the organization. Mark was all of 26 at the time, but I had a good feel for people, their strengths and weaknesses, and I had every confidence that Mark would do well. My confidence proved to be well-founded. He later became one of our most effective vice-presidents, and in 1979, became president of FLEXcon.

Hiring the right people for key roles in a company that is beginning to expand is, as you might expect, critically important. After Mark came aboard I knew I needed to create some other positions and looked to one of my biggest customers, Dennison, for help. Dennison very generously did not stand in the way of opportunity for two young men who wanted to join in our adventure. These two men, Andy Hacanis and Warren Kunz, came to my attention because of the superb way they conducted business for Dennison.

Andy Hacanis was a top salesman for Dennison, a few years older than I was. I was able to observe him often in my interactions with Dennison, especially when I had to pose as a laboratory supervisor for him. Dennison had sold wood-grained pressure-sensitive coverings for radios. GE complained that the coverings kept coming off. Dennison was one of the largest

Bernie Alden, Andy Hacanis and Mark Ungerer, 1986

companies in Massachusetts, occupying much of Framingham, and they did not want GE to know FLEXcon had provided the pressure-sensitive material. So, they asked me to take on the role of a Dennison laboratory supervisor and travel to the GE plant in Syracuse to deal with the problem. I suggested to Jean that we take the boys out of school for a day, make it a long weekend and drive to Niagara Falls. I couldn't show up as "the lab guy" in my new powder blue Cadillac though. Jean had to let me off around the corner so I could walk in, disguise intact. Andy met me, brought me to the problem radios, and we looked them over.

I realized that the silicone the GE guy was using on the mold was causing the pressure-sensitive wood grain covering to fall off. The silicone acted as an anti-sticking agent. All it took was rubbing a little alcohol on it, but we did not want to embarrass GE. We had to work out a team approach to the problem and come to a consensus that indicated GE was as competent as I was to figure it all out. Andy impressed me with his nuances and explanations with the GE guys. He also helped extricate me from lunch and afternoon meetings, so "lab-man" could get back to his family in the new Cadillac. Was my ego damaged? Not at all. Money is money. I'd never let my ego get in the way of money.

Andy and I kept in contact after that incident and by 1969 he wanted to join FLEXcon. I told him I would hire him, but we had to be careful because I did not want to antagonize Dennison by taking one of their top guys. I knew we'd have to play the politics, so I asked him to write me a letter explaining that he wanted to be considered for the position of sales manager. I wrote back saying I appreciated his interest, but I'd have to check with the Dennison people because I'd worked so closely with them all these years. I did indeed talk with his managers and got to acquire a great sales manager and continued the account with Dennison without a hitch.

It was a similar situation with Warren Kunz, the Dennison foreman in charge of silk-screening. Warren knew all about the printing business and could deal with those customers far better than I could. I also wanted him to learn to do our pricing. Through the process of letter-writing and talking to the right people, such as Ashley Van Duser, their sales manager, Warren came to us as well and became invaluable.

I was adding top guys when I didn't have a place for them though. I wasn't ready to spend the money on office space, so we put together a makeshift office. Andy and Warren walled off a space with some two by fours and Mark moved into my office with me. We opened Plant II in 1970 and made enough money to build a 5,000 square foot office in 1971. Finally, everyone who needed an office had one.

Every time I expanded, the old timers would come to me and bitch. They couldn't see why I did it. Maybe I was too accessible to them, but that was the way I wanted it—I wanted to hear what they had to say. When I had only fifteen workers, I'd stop at a restaurant around the corner; get donuts and coffee for everyone, and at 6:00 a.m. I would sit on one of the wrapping tables. They would all know it was time for talk. That's how I found out what was going on. Fifteen minutes was usually enough time to get some problems solved. If I couldn't solve a problem right away, they knew they had some more coffee and donuts coming to them.

Those early morning meetings set a FLEXcon precedent, one that continues to this day: the need and desire for open communication with employees. Loyalty and trust must go both ways between an entrepreneur and his employees. I knew I had to be in touch with my people, to listen to them about pay and bonuses. As the work force expanded it became even more important that they had a direct line to management who would listen and act on their concerns. These meetings were the roots of our Information and Discussion meetings.

I have a very strong opinion about unions, at least unions at, FLEXcon. I did not want them. In fact, I told more than one person if a union came in I would be gone. One simple reason: I wanted to run FLEXcon myself. I did not want other people telling me how to do it. Every once in a while an aggravated employee would try to get a union started. Veteran workers would always squash the idea though. They didn't want any of the negative, adversarial tension that exists in many union-management relationships. My employees knew they had a good thing going for them, they didn't need an outside force, and could speak for themselves—still do.

In the 80s, we began those monthly Information and Discussion meetings. Each department was represented by a worker, on a rotating basis. Once people realized that they would not get fired for speaking their minds, the meetings became very effective, solving all kinds of problems from safety issues to toilet paper shortages. Communication, a key to trust and loyalty, is still a major reason for the positive atmosphere and success of FLEXcon.

Along with learning from my employees, in a similar way, I also began learning from a new organization I joined. The Young Presidents Organization (YPO) was founded many years ago to bring together top young business leaders to discuss mutual problems. At that time potential members had to employ at least fifty people and bring in at least a million dollars in sales annually. These leaders had to be younger than 40 years old and be invited by one member and seconded by another to join. The

Dialogue between employees and management, 1982

potential member would be interviewed, as would his spouse, and if accepted, become eligible to participate in all events. Dick Silverman, of HySil, whom I had done a lot of business with approached me in 1967 about membership in the organization. I was delighted to be invited, FLEXcon had just done its first million the year before, I was thirty-six, and we had fifty employees, at least we did if we counted a couple of spouses.

I remember going to our first meeting in Nantucket aboard a beautiful boat on a sunny summer morning. As we sped along I overheard a conversation between a few of the men. They were discussing the status for membership and all agreed that there was no way you could get to a million in sales unless you had at least fifty employees. I was dying to say that I didn't have fifty,

Members of the Young Presidents Organization, 1985

but my mark-up was so good I still made a million. I had to keep my mouth shut though. Dick had already told me not to worry about fudging the numbers because with the way FLEXcon was growing I'd need over fifty soon, and he was right.

YPO was to become an important part of Jean's and my life. Through YPO we traveled the world, met the heads of governments, and shared social events with many intelligent, articulate business people. Most importantly, I learned so much from my peers and the experts who regularly spoke at our meetings. As business owners, YPO provided us with a sanctuary where we could speak candidly, while respecting one another's privacy. YPO added a university-liberal arts dimension to our lives that we could not have anticipated or found anywhere else. It has been an invaluable educational tool helping me to run and grow FLEXcon.

I served my time in various capacities to become chairman of our chapter and enjoyed all of the connections those jobs offered. I had run the usual treasurer, secretary, education chairman gamut of jobs to become chairman of the New England chapter. Of all the jobs I had in YPO the most demanding and rewarding was that of education chairman. This position must set the agenda for our chapter meetings, select the locale, and do all the logistics of housing and meals. In other words, do more work than any other position. I loved it. I loved running my own show. YPO expanded my personal horizons in ways I would never have been able to do alone. You can be a big fish in a little pond, or try to become a growing fish in a bigger pond, but you have to be around the people whose ideas can expand your own thinking.

The FLEX-who? campaign helped define FLEXcon's image through the 1970s

6

FLEXCON'S EXPANSION

As I said before, I bought most of our equipment at local auctions or scavenged it from area dumps and then built them like erector sets. Once, I found out about a very large oven a company was throwing out that could be of use to me. The oven had been used for flocking, so I had to spend Saturdays cleaning out the damn thing with John Foley's steam machine—filthy, sweaty work. Then I bought a rewind machine from nearby, Hobbs Engineering. The machine was not very precise, but I stubbornly used it for six months. I salvaged the machine by turning it into a gravure coater, which is only one roll over another and doesn't need to be as precise. Erector set construction was fine with me, what would have cost over $50,000 new, cost me only $15,000 and took relatively little time. Well, to be honest, it took almost nine months of hard work to get the machines operative—the very definition of sweat equity.

FLEXcon made its own contributions to the dump too. An operation like ours can develop quite a mess, so dump trips were important for us to keep the place free of debris, sheets of plastic, cardboard, and paper, anything that we could not recycle. Our dump runs were usually around the same time of day.

One day I got word that someone was following our truck into the dump and scavenging through our stuff. I found it a bit ironic because that was exactly what I had done for years. I was concerned it could be someone looking for hints of what we were doing at FLEXcon, helping out the competition. So I trailed our truck into the dump. Sure enough a car followed the truck in and two women with blue scarves on their heads, wearing blue dresses and black shoes got out—nuns. I couldn't believe our competition hired nuns to snoop through our garbage! Or maybe they were just dressed like nuns to avoid looking suspicious. I got out of my car and hurried over to the two, who were pouring through piles of plastic, selecting what they wanted. "Excuse me!" I shouted, "Can I ask you what the hell you two are doing?"

The older one, gray hair leaking out from under her scarf, glared back at me, "We are looking for good plastic materials to use in our school with third graders, if it is any business of yours." They were real nuns! And here I was yelling at them! My anger quickly melted when I saw the situation for what it was. They were just trying to find some useful materials at the dump.

I apologized and said, "Look, why don't we set up a place at FLEXcon where you can come and go through our stuff before we send it here? Take what you'd like in a cleaner place. What do you say?" The two smiled, perhaps surprised that a grouchy business owner would respond this way. Those thieving nuns began a program that exists to this day. Over forty years later teachers still come to a large room in Plant III and find materials they can take back to their schools. They often leave something behind too: Artwork made from FLEXcon cast offs, imaginative uses for material, which otherwise would be just another dump run. FLEXcon contributes more than just material to education in the Spencer area though. We have been happy to provide computers for many classrooms over the years and fund computer specific teacher training.

Plant II constructions brought about a complete change for FLEXcon. The pressure-sensitive business alone created a need for more storage space for raw materials such as Mylar®, vinyl, and paper. To make room we moved laminating out of Plant I, under Norman Collette, to South Spencer Road along with two new coating machines. So, now we had laminating and embossing in Plant II, brushing, coating and Tedlar® in Plant I and the whole first floor on Wall Street for storage. It was fun I will admit, to see changes happening every day and to watch the orders pouring in, the order getting out fast, and the rising of Plant II on South Spencer Road before my eyes. Norman Collette kept thirty to thirty-five guys busy on a top coating machine, a dying machine, four laminators and one pressure-sensitive machine. Back in Plant I, Gerry had twenty going all the time on his machines. Wall Street was overcrowded. South Spencer Road construction had to move and move fast. By that time, 1970, we were on our way to $4 million in sales!

That year we went to the Screen Printing Trade Show in Chicago, a big move for FLEXcon. No one knew who we were. Up until then most of our customer base was in New England

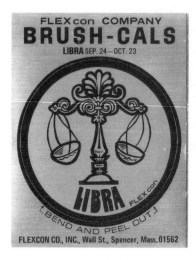

FLEX-who? brushed stainless steel-look zodiac stickers

and a bit in New York. Time to strut our stuff in the big time and spread our name. We printed out some fancy cards—brushed stainless steel laminated to 10 gauge vinyl, with the round zodiac signs below the words "FLEXwhoooo?—and stationed Andy at the entrance inviting people over to our booth. We gave away hundreds of those cards. I also got a suite with a bartender and a lot of people came by for free drinks. Not much serious business discussion because they were all slurping down the freebies, but it was great for networking.

The brushed stainless steel look was a huge hit and potential customers liked our promises of speedy production. Now our horizons started to expand. Yes, I had been to Europe and was still struggling to get that going, but to the Midwest and the South our geography was beginning to expand to include customers from far beyond our self-imposed borders.

The next year at the trade show we introduced another little gimmick. We expanded the idea of FLEX-who? (because no one had heard of us) into the owl; funny though, people were just looking for the Zodiac cards again. So, we were getting publicity with the new owl and for what we did not have—the cards. The impact was almost immediate. We started seeing sales in these new locations across the United States.

Despite our fast turn-around with orders, customers further west began to complain about the time it took to get our deliveries out to Louisiana or Texas. The only way to solve the problem was to have a presence out there. So by 1975 we built our first warehouse in Kansas City, Kansas.

The 70s seemed to go by in a blur of expansion and growth. By 1975 we had reached $10 million in sales and it was decision time. Staying at $10 million is a very nice company. I knew everybody, even knew their kids. We were all making enough money, but in business you either go up or down. I chose to go up—way up. I wanted to take FLEXcon to $100 million over the next ten years. It took us this long, almost twenty years to get to $10 million, yet I had a firm belief that we could do $10 million more each year for the next ten. I had been working on the numbers, looking at the expanding plant, figuring out how we could go after a more diverse market, and I knew we could do it. All I had to do was convince my guys, so I planned a long weekend to discuss it with my top men.

I took Howard Chaphe, who I hired in 1974 to run the lab, Mark Ungerer, Andy Hacanis, and our wives to my condo in

Waterville Valley, New Hampshire, for four days. I wanted to convince my guys that we could reach the $100 million goal, and they wanted to convince me that they should have stock in the company. The previous few years had been phenomenal for FLEXcon and these top employees wanted part of that growth. Stock became the dominant topic, the loudest argument, and the one issue I had to deal with each day of those meetings. Mainly because I said no, there would be no stock opportunities. I would not release stock to anyone. The only way you would ever get stock in FLEXcon was if your name was McDonough. I was adamant about FLEXcon being held entirely by family members. I assured them that they would be paid very well, but no stock. That was my most difficult sell.

I am glad I was stubborn though. Today the family and the company are both doing well. It was my goal at that meeting to set our sights on the $100 million, but also to make it clear that it was my company and it will always be in McDonough hands, every aspect of it. The family has, and always will be, the most important part of FLEXcon.

In 1977 a second member of the family, my wife Jean, came onto the FLEXcon scene. She had a big impact in her own way. She had always been involved in every decision I ever made of course, but now she wanted real responsibility. She had already become a factor on the boards of institutions around Worcester, including the Worcester Art Museum, the EcoTarium, and the Worcester Historical Museum and now she was ready for more. She had seen the amount of money we had saved and thought it was time for that money to go to work for FLEXcon, instead of for the bank. Inflation was up and we were not getting 15% interest or even 14% but the bank was lending its money out at 18%. Jean thought we could do better. We had a meeting with the bank vice president and Jean told them that I didn't seem to know what to do with this money so she was going to be investing it. I was delighted and felt a great relief. I was never interested in investing money. This may sound odd for me to say considering all the years I've spent in the business, but it's true. I'm far more interested in the growth of business than in the growth of money. I didn't want to run the company and then try to pay attention to investing the profits too. I considered them separate jobs and I was very happy that Jean was willing to manage the cash flow.

The bank, however, was not pleased. They were stunned by Jean's proposal, which would empty their vault of a big supply of funds to work with. Jean became so involved that she went into The Management Program at Smith College, which she finished in 1980. The Management Program was started because Smith recognized there were too few women in business school and wanted to help prepare them to participate. Jean was able to go to eight-week summer sessions twice. She worked for FLEXcon for a year and then quit. She didn't like doing all that work for the pay she was getting, which was zero. I was happy to give her a salary though and so she renewed her commitment. A very practical aspect of Jean being so involved concerned my potential demise. If fate somehow intervened and I had died during that time, Jean could have taken over and run the show, until Neil was of sufficient age. In other words, FLEXcon still would

Jean C. McDonough, c. 1980

have remained in the family. Too many family businesses are decimated when the husband/owner suddenly dies.

Jean's decision to take on the job of investing our money came at a very good time. The oil embargo of the early 70s forced a lot of changes in American life, most of them difficult. People had to wait in long lines for gas, only to get half a tank if they were lucky! One good result of the oil embargo was a federal rule that forbade companies to raise prices on any existing oil-based products. New products were exempt though. That meant a great deal to FLEXcon and other small businesses. While our suppliers' prices were frozen, we could charge whatever we wanted. All our products were considered new, and we made money, a lot of money, because everything was marked up, while costs remained the same. None of my customers were mad about it though because they were making more money than we were. Large companies, whose products were well known, could not change a thing, but the government was an unwitting partner of FLEXcon. That and the inflationary standard of currency put us in a very good position for Jean to go to town with her magic investing wand.

FLEXcon was ready and willing to take advantage of the situation. Since the mid-60s, FLEXcon had introduced some important innovations: the brushed stainless steel look, laminates that could be stabilized, film (Mylar®) as release liner in pressure-sensitive materials—using 1 millimeter Mylar® to ensure an inexpensive yet perfectly smooth adherence to glass. All of which contributed to our rapid growth. Mark-ups during the first half of the seventies were probably better than at any other time in all the years I've been in business.

In addition to Jean taking on some of my concerns about investing, Mark Ungerer had become our first Vice President in 1975. He had demonstrated that he could handle people very well and took on the daily interactions with staff, while I concentrated on expanding and growing the business. Mark's responsibility was to take over the meetings and try to figure out the problems that so often bogged me down. I still met with individuals about their problems, but no longer the larger groups. Guys would come to me about money mostly. I learned it is important, in a small company, that no one knows how much the other guy makes. I made it clear that you don't tell anyone how much you are making, no matter what your position is, even among sales people, whose figures are published in regard to their territories and projected goals. If some salesmen thought they should make more, or didn't meet their goals, they would come to me to talk about their situation.

For many years we awarded plaques and incentives to the salesmen who did the best in their territories. If you did two million this year and the year before, you were expected to do three million the next year. It was not that difficult to do a million more in the 70s, much more difficult now. In fact, it's generally more challenging to be in sales now. Sometimes there is little to no commission after a sale has been negotiated down to a lower figure because we have to meet the lower price to set up other opportunities. The salesman might not make anything at all for all the work he's done. Same is true if the customer puts the sale on hold for ninety days or does not pay for a delivered product within the same time. If the salesman wants to make money, I have to make money. He has his reputation to protect, his territory to run and I need the money out of that territory. Salesmen have a base salary now, but they still want to earn that commission.

I must admit that gross profits always looked good in the 70s. The reality was that raw materials at around 63% of our product were our biggest expense. Labor-intensive manufacturers are usually about 45%. We were not labor-intensive, at least not then, so raw materials accounted for so much more of the cost. We also had to contend with other normal business expenses: health insurance which I always insisted to be the best, costs of building, labor, all of which battled the profit margin into lower figures, but we still made money.

In the fall of 1980, despite my growing business, I experienced a personal setback. I woke up one morning and could not get out of bed. I was fifty years old, still doing all kinds of sports and crazy activities. I loved to come home from work in the summer to our lake house, roll up my trousers, and water ski in my business suit. I could go around the lake and end up at the dock without ever getting wet, well most of the time. I had a few aches and pains—most weekenders do, but never anything alarming. Nothing like this, I could not move my head, no warning.

Fortunately for me, three months before, I had accepted a trustee position at Memorial Hospital, the biggest hospital in Worcester at the time. I had not done it with my own health in mind though, but my employees. I had agreed to join the board on the condition that FLEXcon employees were granted priority treatment. This was not a usual request of new trustees. Most of the other people on the board were professionally prominent, the sort of people who could be relied upon to give generously and get other's support, but I was the only one in manufacturing with a large work force. I had over four hundred people, a lot of potential business for them. Beyond good treatment, I wanted to be kept informed. I wanted to know, personally, when someone from FLEXcon checked into Memorial, whether it was an accident, a problem in a plant, or something in off hours, I wanted to know what was wrong. I wanted to be able to call the wife, and tell her if the guy was okay or not. I wanted to know what to say to the family. If an ambulance went from FLEXcon I wanted to know that it got priority and that the person inside got the best care. The hospital would throw monthly informal dinners with the doctors. Not all of the trustees would go, but I made a point of it so I could get to know the doctors. I wanted them to know me. I spent a lot of time developing these relationships for FLEXcon. I got to know the medical staff too well for them not to return my calls. So, when I slumped into the hospital like Quasimodo that day, the hospital treated me well, just as I expected them to treat my employees. Before long I was in the care of a rheumatologist named Bress.

Three days later I was still there, but at least we had an answer. Bress had extracted fluid from my neck and sent it to Atlanta. The diagnosis came back and it was not good. I had ankylosing spondylitis, a term that meant about as much to me then as it probably does to you now. Spondylitis is a chronic inflammation of the spine, which causes pain and stiffness. It can lead to ankylosing, a process that cements the vertebrae together and limits mobility in the spine. Arthritis of the spine basically, or in other words, a royal pain in the neck, but it doesn't stop there. Once it gets going, arthritis can wreak havoc in all kinds of joints and organs. If you see me walk, or look at my hands, or how my head tilts forward, you know what I mean. I am in rare company though, only about 300,000 Americans have ankylosing spondylitis, less than 1%.

Ten days later I was out of the hospital, with my supply of Indocin, an anti-inflammatory pill in hand. Indocin is very affective for AS, as well as other forms of arthritis, but it is one of those NSAIDS (nonsteroidal anti-inflammatory drugs) that can cause serious stomach problems. Most people can tolerate it for about two weeks before their stomachs wave the white flag. I've been on Indocin for over thirty years now and it has helped me immensely. The doctors and I have no idea why it doesn't bother my stomach. The new stuff, Vioxx and Celebrex, do nothing for me though.

By the mid-80s I was still physically active. I'd just pop one more pill, get rid of the pain and keep moving. I did not tell anyone how many pills I was taking. I knew they were bad, all those pills, but I was having more trouble with my neck and hands, so I took more than the doctors told me to. If I could live actively until seventy taking more pills, it was better than living to ninety sitting on my butt.

Soon after the diagnosis I met a young doctor, Katherine Upchurch, who, because I was in such deep pain, began to shoot cortisone into my knees. She has been extremely helpful and I've been with her for over twenty years now. Katherine has a great well-deserved reputation around Boston and she helped put me in contact with Dr. Scott, one of the leading knee replacement specialists in the northeast, to install my two artificial knees in the mid-90s. To have Dr. Scott's services you usually got in line and stayed there for almost nine months, but Katherine helped me skip the line. Scott did my first knee in 1994, and the second in '96. In both cases I had spinal blocks and watched the operations on the monitor. Soon I was up and going, happily adjusting to walking without wincing every step, but sports were out of the picture. But I had plenty to do at FLEXcon to keep me busy.

I was never angry about my arthritis. You have to accept it and do the best you can. I once went to visit a guy in the hospital who had been paralyzed in a construction accident. The whole time I was there he kept asking me to scratch his back, or his neck, or some other place. He couldn't scratch himself. It made me feel so grateful that I could move. My hands may not be pretty, but at least when I have an itch I can scratch it!

Arthritis has led me to become involved with the Arthritis Foundation. Katherine Upchurch unashamedly pesters me for research donations and support, which I am, of course, happy to give. I also sponsor some activities here in Worcester for others with arthritis. Once a year Jean and I invite ninety or so people affected by arthritis to come to an all day meeting, at which doctors speak on different aspects of living with the disease and coping with all the complications it can bring. Then we give them lunch and have therapists offer practical advice during the afternoon session.

There is a Walk for Arthritis fundraiser every year at the school my grandchildren attend, Bancroft. Over the years I have also helped organize a breakfast at the Worcester Club hosting some of Worcester's best, to raise interest, awareness, and of course, money for an arthritis cure.

Myles began to suffer from severe arthritis of the spine in 1980. Far from slowing down, he became involved in supporting the Arthritis Foundation while running FLEXcon. This photo was taken circa 2005.

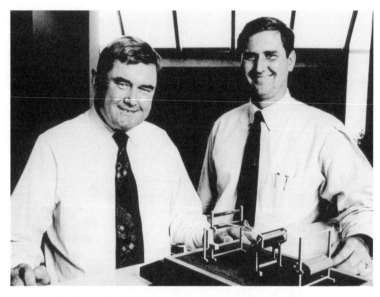

Myles and Neil McDonough with a replica of FLEXcon's
first laminating machine, 1992

Spencer campus of FLEXcon, 2016
Courtesy of K&J Benjamin Photography, 2016

7

THE 100 MILLION DOLLAR GOAL

In 1981 MY SON Neil joined FLEXcon. He had graduated from Trinity College, in Hartford, Connecticut, and received his MBA from Babson. I hired him, at the age of twenty-four, as a salesman. I had always believed that the second generation in a family business has to begin in sales. If you are born rich then you don't know how to kiss ass, and you had better learn how to in sales or you'll never make it as an executive. I assigned Neil to the northern New England territory and he proved to be a natural salesman. He quickly learned to be the most pleasant person a buyer has to deal with. He would come in with one new product and always promise to bring something new again next time. It kept the buyer wanting to see him. It didn't take Neil long to earn the FLEXcon $2 million plaque for annual sales.

Around the same time, David Mielcarz, a Williams graduate, came to FLEXcon. I recognized him as a bright guy and made him Marketing Manager. Before him, marketing at FLEXcon had been pretty simple: get the customer and keep him. Mielcarz came in and established a new philosophy. Up to that point we had depended upon the customer to think of new ways to use us. Mielcarz wanted us to expand our horizons, be more proactive in going after new customers, companies that didn't even think they would want our products.

One of the most significant developments during the early 80s was the transition from sheet labeling to roll labeling. Sheet labeling, used in such products as clock facings and washing machine name plates, demands thick release paper that lays flat with the material.

Once die-cut the release paper has to be taken off by hand, a very time consuming process. Roll labeling uses thin release paper instead, so it can be die cut more easily and efficiently. In this process a machine is used to peel off the release paper, saving time and energy.

As with all new materials and techniques, roll labeling required a lot of lab tests. At this point Plant I was nostalgically being kept as a relic, but it found use again as the home of these experiments. The machines kept in Plant I were significantly slower than our others, so we could work out any problems on a smaller scale. The machine moved the roll at about eighteen to twenty yards per minute. If we found any problems with adhesives or if it wrinkled we could easily stop the machine. Once it passed the tests of Plant I we would move on to Plant II. There the machines were double to triple the speed, so we could see if the process held up. Next it would move to Plant IV, where the speed was doubled yet again. These experiments saved us a lot of time and, because we could quickly stop the slower machines

Spencer Plant II clean room interior, 2014

and not waste product, saved us a lot of money. When we were finally convinced that the product was a go, we would run it in Plant V at a hundred yards per minute.

Silk screen and pressure sensitive products had brought us to fifty million in sales at that point, but going to roll label was about to increase orders dramatically and become an important aspect of getting us to our stated $100 million goal. We were delivering products customers had never seen before.

Eventually we were selling about two times more in roll labels than in sheet. One of the keys to our productivity was the innovation of Flexographic printing. Previously, gravure printing had used four to six engraved cylinders. The process was extremely time-consuming because each roll could only transfer one color, and then the sheet had to be dried completely, before the next cylinder applied a new color. Flexography completely revolutionized the process because the ink would transfer directly from a steel roll to a rubber roll, which applied the design much like the imprint of a hand-held rubber stamp, eliminating the dry time.

However, our advantages in using Flexography were far greater than just its efficiency. A gravure cylinder cost about $3,000, while a Flexographic rubber cylinder cost about $500. FLEXcon's strength has always been to bring in a variety of customers by offering them unique solutions, and also by accommodating their needs for shorter runs. The less expensive cylinders of Flexographic printing meant we could afford to keep satisfying smaller orders and still make money. Another important advantage was the ease of re-engraving rubber rolls, as opposed to the three week wait for a gravure cylinder.

With these new innovations we were quickly gaining on my goal of one hundred million in sales. To help inspire my men I turned to a new bird, besides our FLEXwhoooo owl, Jonathan Livingston Seagull. He was the protagonist bird of the book by Richard Bach. I bought three cases of the book and three seagull replicas for a big sales meeting in Puerto Rico. Unlike most of his peers who want to know only the basics about flying—to get food mainly, young Jonathan loved to fly. The flying was more important to him than the eating, spending time off by himself, hungry, but happy because he was learning. He kept pushing far beyond what seagulls are supposed to do and kept going for new speed records with sometimes accidental and painful results. He found new ways to fly faster, bringing him joy, power, and beauty. His passion and skills lifted him out of ignorance. His

Statue of Jonathan Livingston Seagull, from the book by Richard Bach.
The story was a great inspiration to Myles.
(Left to right) *Mark Ungerer, Myles, Bernie Alden, 1986*

new powers rewarded him with new adventures, better food and new ways of thinking. Bach becomes more philosophical, in a 70s kind of way, in the rest of the book: If we can think it, we can do it, that sort of thing, but it was the first part that really caught my attention. For me, the excitement of moving FLEXcon forward with such rapid success was a lot like Jonathan learning to take on higher and higher speeds of flying.

He's only a seagull. He's supposed to grub around for morsels of food from fishing boats or garbage pails. Instead, he gets his fun from trying to see how high he can go and breaking his limits. FLEXcon, for me, was somewhat the same. Don't get me wrong, I liked the money, but I worked hard for it. We all did. The excitement was the flying, the speed, the attempt at higher and higher flight, constantly pushing our boundaries and defying the limits. That's what I wanted my salesmen to feel as well, and I think they did. I think that seagull had a lot to do with us getting to the $100 million goal.

We reached the $100 million in sales mark in 1985. Jean commissioned a wood sculpture of a seagull that sat on my desk for some time to remind me of Jonathan and the hard work it took to reach my goal. By the next year I was worn out and needed a break though. As fate would have it, Neil had moved to head of marketing and was ready for more, as was Bernie Alden. They both wanted to reach $200 million, Neil because he was just starting out as an executive and Bernie because he wanted to reach it before he retired. I said go for it, I'll watch.

IMPRESSIONS & MEMORIES OF MYLES

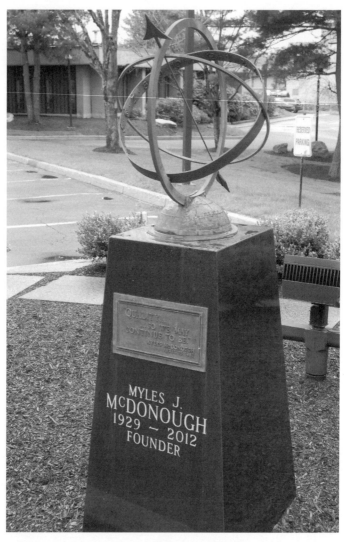

Memorial sundial outside the Myles McDonough building at FLEXcon's headquarters. The inscription from a quote by Myles reads:
"Quality ... so we may continue to be."

In this chapter a small collection of FLEXcon employees and close friends recount their memories of Myles and what made him a successful entrepreneur.

—————

Shirley Cummings came to FLEXcon to work in payroll in the 70s and stayed for twenty-five years. As the company expanded so did Shirley's duties, rising to the position of head of Human Resources. Shirley recalls when she first experienced the culture of FLEXcon:

One day I saw Myles come into our little supply closet with a pad of paper. It had a few pages left in it, not many. "First time I ever saw anyone put something back," I joked.

"That's because I pay for them," he retorted. By that time, Myles could have bought twenty pads and never thought about it for a second, but it had always been part of the FLEXcon culture to be thrifty. I believe that was a big part of Myles' success. He wasn't cheap, but he was always on top of what he did. "Spend the money as if it were your own," he would say.

The people in the shop trusted Myles implicitly because he always did what he said he'd do. They might not always like what he said, but he always told them the truth and when you are in manufacturing, the truth is important. Not all bosses tell their workers the truth. Often they tell them what they want to know, if Myles told you something, you knew it was true. Trust comes from that.

If employees know you care, they'll work twice as hard for you. If they think you could care less, then they develop a different attitude. If, for example, Myles is out in the plant and asks Joe how his son is doing in college, then Joe knows his boss cares. Myles was a business man and if you screwed up you'd be told, but he cared about all his people. In my position in HR, I could see the fierce loyalty he got in return. Loyalty and admiration are not given out lightly by people working hard in manufacturing, but when their work is appreciated it means so much more.

Loyalty between owner and worker, a culture of thrift, and efficient money management are all qualities I saw at FLEXcon in my twenty-five years working there. Maybe they weren't the only ingredients for success, but they were certainly important factors.

Jerry Fitzsimons spent twenty-five years at FLEXcon, mostly in customer service. Before joining FLEXcon, he was able to watch the development of the company from the point of view of a customer, working for Markham. He remembers Myles' loyalty to customers and the community:

At Markham I did business with some of FLEXcon's competitors, but it didn't take me long to understand why FLEXcon was growing so much faster. When FLEXcon made a promise they kept it. If an order was going to be even one day late, you'd get a call. No bad surprises. What they said is what they did.

When I started working at FLEXcon I found that they treated their community just as well as their customers. Local kids out of high school applied at FLEXcon and we hired a great many of them, but our interaction with the town went even further. Myles' "Bonus Bucks" was a program that encouraged employees and also supported the community. If we hit our sales goal for the month we all got a certificate worth a certain amount of money. Myles believed strongly in supporting local business, therefore these certificates could only be used in local stores. I, for one, earned enough certificates over two years to paint my whole house outside and in. Myles' support didn't stop there though. He would buy FLEXcon supplies locally as well. There were probably better prices to be had from larger suppliers in Worcester or Boston, but, when he could, he was determined to give his business to Spencer. It has been a very fast twenty-five years with memories of great people to work with and so many good friends.

ANDY HACANIS had been at Dennison for ten years before he came to FLEXcon in 1969. At Dennison, Andy questioned often and found ways to improve that were ignored by management. He saw what he considered policies and attitudes that did not promote growth. He knew he needed change. After a call from Myles and the sales manager, Andy joined FLEXcon and spent twenty-nine years there, enjoying every minute:

When I came to FLEXcon in 1969, I was ready for anything. It was a relatively new company, with few employees and new products, poised to take on the future. Fortunately for me, Dennison had brought in Ashley van Deuser the year before. Ashley was enthusiastic, intelligent, and vastly knowledgeable about any plastic product you could name. He knew his stuff and loved to talk about it. I loved to listen, to take in all he had to say. That was fortunate for me because I was armed with a lot of knowledge before I even came to FLEXcon. Mark Ungerer talked me into joining FLEXcon; it was not a hard sell though. In fact I agreed to come before I even knew my compensation. Call it a great leap of faith. When I met with Myles to finalize my job as a salesman, I asked him if he was going to stay in business for the long run or make a few bucks and get out. After all, I had five kids to feed. "I intend to build a viable business in the industry," he said, "As long as we're having fun and making money, we'll be in business," that was all I needed to hear.

I soon found out that FLEXcon did not have executives, but people who executed. Myles set the pace. He swore like a trooper, but because he bent down to pick up a stray piece of paper off the floor, so did we. As time went on I loved what I did at FLEXcon. I felt very comfortable from day one. It never felt like work— quite a contrast from my previous job. If I had to fly to Toronto and hit five cities in two days and I had to be away, it didn't bother me. It was always a great challenge.

FLEXcon was a pioneer in so many ways with methods, products, and materials. I think the freedom we had as employees to execute, experiment, and follow through was a key to that pioneering spirit. One day Myles was in my office. The phone rang and he said, "Hold on a second, the goddamn sales manager is right here," and handed me the phone. Nothing special you might say, but it was my job, in my office and he was not going to interfere. We always had the freedom to execute. I could make decisions in the field because I knew our products, the mark-ups and the profit margins. I could decide without having to get permission from someone else.

When we first went to the trade shows in Chicago, we broke all kinds of rules, probably because we didn't realize there were any rules. Our competition didn't really know how to handle us at first. So many of them were paper oriented and paper skilled, they had to buy from us what they could not make themselves. We'd try anything from materials for shoes to interiors of air-planes. If it looked like wood, glass metal, or fabric we could duplicate the look on low-cost durable plastic. We'd sell to any-one—and particularly enjoyed selling to our competitors.

One of our most effective pioneering methods was our sample department. We had to get our samples to potential customers. How else would they know if we could make what they wanted? On the road I'd pick up the phone and say please send out today, or tomorrow at the latest, x numbers of sheets or rolls of the ex-act material a customer was looking for. Our competitors would come in with a few 8 x 10 sheets. We would have fifty sheets, 27 x 20 which the customer could take right to the machine and maybe print out a whole job, and because they were samples, it cost them nothing. Then the customer would buy from us. Even if we sent them rolls of samples rather than a number of sheets, it paid off for us. Sampling gave us the opportunity to show the customer how our product compared to others.

Another important decision Myles made early on had to do with release paper, the paper you peel off to make the pressure-sensitive material stick. The release paper is as important to the success of a product as the product itself, something we found out the hard way. We were using 78-pound mando liner for our release paper. When the product went through the ovens to laminate the film material to the vinyl, the vinyl would shrink a bit. When you put that into roll form and cut it into sheets the whole thing would curl up. If it was winter or a low humidity the customer might have gotten lucky with some sheets remaining flat, but once he added his layers of heavy ink printing and put it through his own ovens to dry, FLEXcon had big problems and complaints came pouring in.

Our competitors were selling a 90 pound poly liner with a special coating which was heavy enough to avoid the curling. We had no choice, but to change. Myles made the decision quickly and also decided to keep our price the same as before, although it was costing us more to invest in the heavier liner. As a result, we overwhelmed the competition. None of our competitors could believe we could sell the product at that price and still make money. We did it through volume, fast sampling and delivery strategies, and the promise that if the product didn't work the customer got his money back, even shipping costs. We lost money at first, but Myles nipped the problem early enough. A new supplier, fewer reruns and refunds and things started to take off.

Another contributor to FLEXcon's success was a new topcoat. Many films were very difficult to work with because the ink didn't want to stick to smooth surfaces, such as vinyl, and they chipped off. FLEXcon developed new topcoats, one for vinyl, and another for polyester, our bread and butter products. Customers in a variety of industries such as the sheet form screen process industry, and the Flexo industry found out that they could use a variety of inks and use our products without fear of flaking. We became popular with offset printing people and the letter press guys, who used a wide range of inks. We were in demand to print screen trade shows. I'd make presentations before 150 to 300 people. They all wanted us because we could make their everyday jobs relatively easy to do.

When customers used our products with the new topcoats, they soon realized they could broaden their product lines, creating more business for FLEXcon. The more products customers had, the more they needed us. To give FLEXcon a great advantage, we could sell customers products in screen set or off set and at half the price of our competitors.

There were other important contributions to FLEXcon's growth: FLEXcon's efficient sampling and fast turnaround for orders continued to do their job, our release paper gave us great results and very few recalls, and customer service remained a top priority. A customer always got an answer on the phone—a "Good morning" and a name to go with the voice. To get our orders out that much faster, Warren Kunz handled sheet form orders and Ed McDade dealt with roll form. Warren, by the way, set the precedent with his skill in pricing for profit. He had come from Dennison before me. (Mark hired him away from my department with my permission, of course), and knew plastic products and their end uses very well. He was always able to nail a profitable price. I think Myles liked Warren very much.

Another important component in FLEXcon's growth was the personality appraisal program that tested every new hire to match prospective employees to specific jobs. I was surprised at first at how successful the questionnaire was in determining the success of an interview and later success on the job, but I quickly learned that it was one of the most important factors of our success. FLEXcon was able to match the candidate with a specific job or position, given the traits displayed in the testing. That made FLEXcon more efficient because people were placed where they could be most effective.

All of these factors: the sampling process, the orders out quickly, the good sales strategies, the superior release paper and topcoats, the attention to customer service, and the personal appraisal program, all whirling around at top speed, in a spirit of fun and excitement, led to FLEXcon's mushrooming success.

———

Pete Robbins started working at FLEXcon at age 20 in the Kansas City warehouse. He was impressed by Myles the first time he met him:

I was a young kid, 22 years old, working for FLEXcon in Kansas City when Myles came out for a visit. I went out to his hotel to pick him up and we had a 45 minute ride to the warehouse. He immediately asked me about my ideas for this operation. I had just two years of experience and the owner was asking my opinions and advice. He unabashedly shared his hopes for FLEXcon and listened to my ideas. His obvious attention to employees gave me such a feeling of encouragement and empowerment. By the end of that car ride I knew I would put my head through a wall to help that man succeed.

Myles was always encouraging and supporting his employees. One time he watched as I flipped through the yellow pages trying to find potential customers. He excitedly told me, "That's how I used to do it! This is the fun part of business!" Twenty-five years later, in a meeting about an inside sales effort I had started, other employees were expressing their disapproval of the idea. It was going to be off site and people did not like that. Myles slipped me a note that said, "Don't worry about them, we both know the power of the yellow pages." I couldn't believe he still remembered that old sales tactic. In a time when so many others were criticizing my idea it felt good to have Myles' support.

In the early 80s one of my favorite FLEXcon urban legends started about Myles because of a particularly frustrating customer. As the story goes, Myles and the customer got in a huge screaming match over a $7 million debt, pushing Myles to yell: "I'm too old and too rich for this shit!" and storm out. The reality of the story is much less dramatic, but shows a lot about Myles' business mentality. At the time we were offering a special 1% discount for customers that paid within ten days of order placement. Terry Van Der Tuuk of Graphic Technical Inc., a bombastic entrepreneur, was taking the discount, but paying 23 to 45 days later. Over time he had racked up quite a debt, around $80,000 due to these "discounts." When Myles found out about the way he was taking advantage of the discount program he was pissed and wanted to cut Terry as a client altogether. It wasn't the money that upset him; it was the disregard for their professional relationship. That wasn't the way we did business in Myles' building. FLEXcon has a strong moral code, and as much as we valued Terry as a customer, we couldn't do business with someone that violated that code. I told Myles we couldn't cut him entirely though, we had too much inventory, it would be better to wean him off, and so we flew out to Kansas City for a meeting with Terry to figure out how to move forward. Terry explained that he felt he did not owe anything and Myles explained that he most certainly did and that he had better pay up or they would be going their separate ways. There was a thick tension in the air, but I never expected what Myles said next. In a stern yet very matter of fact tone, he uttered his now famous line: "I'm too old and too rich to put up with this shit." It was not a challenge or an insult, but a completely genuine moment of spontaneity, in which Myles was able to express his feelings of disappointment and frustration with Terry. Luckily Terry understood the nature in which this remark was intended and conciliatorily agreed to pay the debt. Myles' honest approach to the situation had won Terry's respect and a large check. I remember driving away feeling very relieved and having a good chuckle with Myles about the look of surprise on Terry's face.

That urban legend and the exclamation at its core have come to represent FLEXcon's no-nonsense approach to business. We treat customers fairly and expect the same in return. By the way, we ended up keeping Terry on as a customer and Myles and he sustained a long and open business relationship after that incident.

....

Tom Jacques was in manufacturing at FLEXcon for forty-three years:

Why do people stay with FLEXcon so long? In addition to all the health care and personal concern Myles showed, there are many other reasons, some simple, some more complicated. Take, for example, Christmas bonuses. Myles decided to give out these bonuses the day before Thanksgiving, rather than Christmas, that way employees had some money to shop with. Simple enough to do, but it created an enormous impact on people who depended on that bonus.

Bonus Bucks was another simple idea. These were certificates, worth $10, earned through motivational programs tied to production, sales goals, quitting smoking, or some other recognition. Bonus Bucks could be brought to any retailer in Spencer and spent like real money. At the end of the month the merchants turned them into FLEXcon and got cash. Often, of course, our people would go into a store and spend more than just their certificate. So, you have two groups benefitting from the Bonus Bucks, our employees and Spencer merchants. It was a good way to help the community. Speaking of community, Myles made it a point to purchase as much of our supplies as he could from local suppliers. It might have cost him a little more to buy 200 or so pallets from the local lumber yard, but Spencer loved the business, and we didn't have to stock hundreds of them from a big supplier who would only take big orders. We could just call them when we needed more. The townspeople loved us: we employed a hell of a lot of them and the merchants did well too.

FLEXCON 60 YEARS

THIS TIMELINE was originally published in 1996 in a Special 40th Anniversary Supplement of the FLEXcon newsletter, *FLEXible Converter.* Recent milestones are added through 2016.

1956   Myles McDonough invests $15,000 and opens FLEXcon Company in Spencer, MA.

1959   FLEXcon outgrows its space and moves to new headquarters on Wall Street.

1959

1960   An addition is built to house more machines. Eventually, Myles buys the old wood building next door, and tears it down for further FLEXcon expansion.

1960

Myles Processing is founded, a company that dyes metallized polyester films. Norman Collette manages the manufacturing operation.

1962   Vari-Coating, a company that applies pressure-sensitive adhesives to film products is founded with Gerry Collette, Norma's brother, managing the manufacturing operation.

1962

1965   Myles Processing, Vari-Coating and FLEXcon merge to become FLEXcon Company, Inc.

1966   FLEXcon achieves $1 million in sales.

1969   FLEXcon outgrows Wall Street facility; Myles buys 35 acres on South Spencer Road and breaks ground for a second plant.

1969

1972   Administrative and accounting personnel move into new office building connected to Plant II.

1974   FLEXcon achieves $10 million in sales.

Plant III is completed and houses a finishing plant, warehouse and offices for freight transportation, the New Ventures team, safety and environmental, and computer operations.

The European Headquarters is established at Weesp (Netherlands).

1976   Distribution centers in Kansas and Canada open.

1978   The Georgia distribution center opens.

1979   "Tell me again why we built a building this big ..."
Plant IV, which will provide growth for the 80s
and beyond, is completed. It houses manufacturing,
quality engineers, business teams, and quality and
applications laboratories.

The California distribution center opens.

1981 "We are proud to be part of your team." Employees congratulate Myles and Jean as FLEXcon celebrates is 25th anniversary.

1982 Massachusetts Governor Edward King presents FLEXcon the President's "E" Award in recognition of outstanding contribution to the company's increase in overseas trade.

1983   The North Branford, CT, facility comes on line.

1984   Myles is the The Association of International Metallizers, Coaters and Laminators (AIMCAL) "Man of the Year."

The Minnesota plant is procured.

1985   FLEXcon achieves $100 million in sales.

The annex to Plant IV becomes a functional addition.

1986   "Do It Right the First Time, Every Time."
FLEXcon enters Total Quality Process with Philip
Crosby Associates.

My Pledge To
Quality Improvement

that I will make a conscious eff___ to c
first time every day. I recogniz___ t m___
benefit me personally and wi___ ___i___
continued success.

1986

A groundbreaking ceremony is held for the
Corporate Office Building.

1986

1988   Employees move into new space in the Myles McDonough Corporate Office Building.

1989   The Wisconsin distribution center opens.

FLEXcon receives the "Quality Fanatic Recognition Award" from Philip Crosby Associates, Inc., honoring companies for their enthusiasm in adopting the quality improvement program.

1990   Neil McDonough is named President of FLEXcon.

The Ohio distribution center opens.

Plant V is completed, adding manufacturing space and connecting Plants III and IV.

1991 The completion of Plant VI, off Bixby Road, brings the total manufacturing and warehouse space in FLEXcon's Industrial Park to more than 600,000 square feet.

1992 FLEXcon achieves $200 million in sales.

1993 A new manufacturing facility is built on 60 acres in Columbus, Nebraska.

1994   Meeting world-class quality standards: FLEXcon achieves ISO 9001 certification.

1995-1998   "Partners Preventing Hazards." FLEXcon receives safety awards from OSHA's Voluntary Protection Program (VPP) for achieving Merit and STAR status. FLEXcon became involved with VPP to enhance the safety process and build its safety culture.

1996   FLEXcon celebrates its 40th anniversary.

1997   FLEXcon Europe builds a plant in Glenrothes, Scotland with adhesive and top coating capabilities to support customer growth in Europe. Weesp, Netherlands remains the front end and distribution to the continent. Adding application development and full coating capabilities ensured that FLEXcon could continue to grow regional share.

1999-2000   Groundbreaking and opening of Plant II in Columbus, NE, doubles the square footage to 400,000, and combines the manufacturing and distribution needs for our customers west of the Mississippi into one major operation.

2002   FLEXcon embarks on the "lean" manufacturing journey, a systematic approach to identifying and eliminating waste through continuous improvement by following the product at the demand of the customer. The result has been increased responsiveness, expansion of competitive advantage, and sustained sales and earnings growth.

2007   FLEXcon Kentucky (Elkton Plant) opens, an adhesive coating plant designed to support one major customer and the labeling of glass & PET containers. By dedicating an asset and manufacturing plant to a single-customer focus, FLEXcon was able to experiment with and better understand lean manufacturing principles.

2007

2010-11   The Tech Center brings all of R&D under one roof in a collaborative environment. The open office environment of the Tech Center and close proximity between all the teams resulted in the opportunity for immediate dialogue and brainstorming on projects.

2011   FLEXcon purchases California based Arlon Graphics, a coater of cast vinyl and digital print films. With this acquisition, FLEXcon expanded its product portfolio in advertising and promotional products, as well as extending its sales channel and global market presence.

2011   ECP is acquired and renamed FLEXcon Industrial, in San Antonio, TX. A market leader in several niche segments, FLEXcon Industrial shares synergies with FLEXcon including a commitment to innovation, lean manufacturing/sustainability, ISO, dedication to employees, customers, suppliers and the greater community.

2012   FLEXcon Asia opens in Hong Kong for laminating and slitting. These two capabilities enable FLEXcon to level the competitive landscape and meet the regional standard for lead times. In addition, FLEXcon Asia offers regional Tech Service Engineering allowing a fine tuning of product constructions to meet specific customer application requirements.

2014   FLEXcon purchases SMV Technologies—a fluorescent PVC manufacturer—and moves to San Antonio, TX, location with FLEXcon Industrial SMV Technologies strengthened FLEXcon's industrial products with highly fluorescent films sold worldwide under its Stabrite® brand.

2016   FLEXcon rebrands. Recommitting to our purpose —to help our customers to make the most of their opportunities and achieve their potential. Our purpose includes helping FLEXcon employees "become more than they thought they could be."

*In 2015, Jean McDonough received the key to the
City of Worcester for her philanthropy.*

*The McDonough family (from left): Dylan, Kelsey, Mark, Jean,
Neil, Caitlin with Mara, Lisa, Shaun*
Missing from photo: *Darcy, Ryan, Lillie, Mike Mackenzie,
Cait McDonough, Landon*

ACKNOWLEDGEMENTS

THIS BOOK would never have been started and restarted without a push from my wife Jean. She found and hired Jack Galvin of WriteJack Writing Services, who proved to be an excellent listener, questioner, and writer. Jack has prepared my stories for my grandchildren, Caitlin, Shaun, Ryan, Kelsey, Lillie, Darcy, and Dylan, and their children, Mara, Landon, and undoubtedly more to come. I hope my story may inspire each of you to persevere when following your dreams—and maybe even lead FLEXcon into the future. I am also glad to share my story with all others who may be interested in this great American success story.

I thank my granddaughter Darcy for picking up the rough manuscript and giving it a first edit. Of course, a finished book requires professional midwifery. TidePool Press, Ingrid Mach and Jock Herron, have played that role, guiding this project to the finish line.

Finally, a great thank you to my FLEXcon Family. They have given me so much through the years, and I see so much that's positive in FLEXcon's future. I always wanted to build an enduring business—a family business. My humblest thanks go to the Pioneer Club as I started, in 1991, to call the six of us who had the faith and put in the sweat and hours to grow this company from its birth, through its adolescent years into adulthood. Allen R. Fontaine, David C. Ingalls, Thomas E. Jacques, Myles McDonough, Kenneth L. Phoenix, and Philip M. Rhault are the members of FLEXcon's Pioneer Club. And yes, I include myself as a member; it has always been a team effort.

Myles J. McDonough